TOUGH
INTERVIEW
QUESTIONS
and how to
ANSWER
THEM

Rachel Adamson and Mandy Soule are co-founders and directors of The Assessment Partnership (www.tapuk.biz), a consultancy that provides advice and practical support to private and public sector businesses in the areas of assessment, selection and development of their people.

Rachel has a retail and financial services background and as a consultant and resourcing manager has specialised in the use of behavioural competencies in the selection and management of staff as well as leading the development of recruitment processes and strategies.

Mandy has an engineering and financial services background and is qualified in the use of a range of psychometric tools to support the development and assessment of staff at all levels. As a consultant and HR professional she has extensive experience in the design of innovative assessment processes and training techniques.

which?

TOUGH
INTERVIEW
QUESTIONS
and how to
ANSWER
THEM

**Rachel Adamson
and Mandy Soule**

Essex County Council Libraries

Which? Books are commissioned and published by Which? Ltd,
2 Marylebone Road, London NW1 4DF
Email: books@which.co.uk

Distributed by Littlehampton Book Services Ltd,
Faraday Close, Durrington, Worthing, West Sussex BN13 3RB

British Library Cataloguing in Publication Data
A catalogue record for this book is available from the British Library

ISBN 978 1 84490 069 5

1 3 5 7 9 10 8 6 4 2

Although the authors and publishers endeavour to make sure the information in this book is accurate and up-to-date, it is only a general guide. Before taking action on financial, legal, or medical matters you should consult a qualified professional adviser, who can consider your individual circumstances. The authors and publishers cannot accordingly accept liability for any loss or damage suffered as a consequence of relying on the information contained in this guide.

Acknowledgements
The authors would like to thank Saville Consulting (www.savilleconsulting.com) for giving us permission to use their sample tests; Belbin Associates (www.belbin.com) for giving us permission to use their team role descriptions; and Jit Jethwa from i3 Consultancy for his equality and diversity advice.

Project manager: Kim Gilmour
Edited by Emma Callery
Designed by Bob Vickers
Index by Lynda Swindells
Printed and bound by Charterhouse, Hatfield

Baskerville Offset is an elemental chlorine-free paper produced using timber from sustainably managed forests. The mill is ISO14001 and EMAS certified.

For a full list of Which? Books, please call 01903 828557, access our website at www.which.co.uk, or write to Littlehampton Book Services. For other enquiries call 0800 252 100.

Contents

Introduction

We find ourselves in a rapidly changing job market. It is one that is increasingly competitive with many applications for each vacancy and employers looking for a wide variety of skills and qualities. Even methods of interviewing and selection have changed, with many more employers using assessment centres or structured competency based interviews to choose the right people to join their business.

In such a challenging environment it is critical that you are able to stand out from the crowd, demonstrate your skills, experiences and qualities effectively and answer interview questions confidently. This book could be the secret to your success – with over 400 interview questions it will give you an understanding of the questions you may be asked and valuable guidance on how to answer them. In addition, there is a chapter dedicated to assessment centres explaining what they are, what to expect and how to prepare for them (see pages 226–37).

This book is written by recruitment professionals who work with organisations of all types and sizes in the public and private sectors and across all industries. As such it provides a realistic guide to the questions that are being asked by employers and ones that they want to hear a good answer to. Some of the questions included are not necessarily good practice, but you may well be asked them, so you need to be prepared for these and have thought about how you will handle them.

What does a modern employer want?

Employers look for a variety of different skills and qualities when they recruit new staff or promote existing ones, but increasingly they are focusing upon appointing individuals who demonstrate the right attitudes, behaviours and personal qualities to deliver in the role rather than simply selecting someone who has the technical skills or knowledge for the position. The belief is that skills and knowledge can be taught or developed if need be, whereas it will be more difficult, or even impossible, to change the way that someone goes about his or her job or interacts with colleagues and customers.

Another question interviewers ask themselves these days when assessing a candidate is, 'Does this person fit with the culture of our organisation?' For example, if their organisation is very focused upon team working, they will want to be sure that this is something that a prospective employee is good at, enjoys and wants to be part of. There is nothing worse than finding out too late that the latest recruit is much more effective working independently and struggles to make decisions with others.

It is also important for many employers to be convinced that applicants have a genuine motivation for wanting to work for their organisation and don't just see this as simply another application. In a competitive market when there are many applicants for a role, this can be a critical aspect for a recruiting manager – it would be much better to select someone who has a genuine interest in their organisation and wants to get really involved in what is going on there.

What is an interview all about?

An interview is simply a way for a prospective employer to gather information about candidates, and to understand their skills, experiences, knowledge and approach to work. It is a way of bringing to life the information you provided them with in your CV or application form, an opportunity to sell yourself and for both the interviewer and you to assess whether or not the job and organisation are right for you.

Most interviews are not designed to trip you up, make you feel uncomfortable or give you a grilling. Yes, good interviewers will want to make a thorough assessment of the candidates that have been short listed, but the interviewers also want to create a positive impression – after all, they will want one of the candidates to accept the job when offered it.

You should see an interview as your opportunity to sell yourself to the organisation and do this by answering all the questions thoroughly, confidently and concisely.

What next?

The most important thing you can do before attending an interview is preparation. Of course, no one can tell you exactly what questions they will ask, what approach they will take to conducting the interview or what skills and qualities they will concentrate upon, but these are all things that you can take an educated guess about by looking at the range of information you have about the job.

Using this book, work through the opening general chapters and then select the ones that relate most closely to your situation or job requirements. Doing this will ensure that you go into the interview well prepared having given real thought to your skills and qualities and unique selling points. You owe it to yourself to do this – you wouldn't make a public speech, presentation or attend an important meeting without preparing, so why would you try to wing it in an interview?

Preparation is one of the easiest ways of reducing the nerves that strike most of us in a pressured situation like an interview – you are much more likely to be able to think of good answers and strong examples if you have already worked thorough some of these prior to the interview.

This book is designed to support you through the process of preparing for an interview. Read through it and pick out the sections relevant to yourself, the job you have applied for or the kind of interview you are expecting. The opening chapters guide you through how and what information to prepare followed by Chapters 3–10, which cover questions that you may be asked in the interview. Chapter 11 focuses on questions you can ask the interviewer. Chapter 12 is about assessment centres and gives comprehensive insight into what these are about and how to prepare for them.

The authors regularly work with a range of job hunters offering training and support in preparation for interviews and assessment centres. In doing so, they have developed a good understanding of the real concerns of candidates and the appropriate mechanisms that can be used by them to prepare effectively and make the best presentation of their skills, qualities and potential for the role they have applied for.

The interview process can be a stressful and challenging time for many, but also a good opportunity for you to take stock of your own skills and qualities and think about what you want out of your working life. Throughout the book you will find a range of hints and tips to make your preparation and interview experience as positive and stress free as possible.

1 Preparation

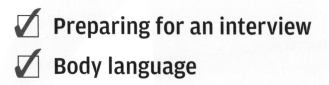

☑ Preparing for an interview
☑ Body language

Preparing for an interview

This chapter covers the importance of preparing for an interview and the key things you can do to ensure you will be able to answer questions fluently and with confidence. It may seem a tedious or boring activity but preparation is the most important thing you can do before attending for an interview for a variety of reasons, including:

- Helping reduce anxiety if you feel under pressure in the interview.
- Focusing your mind on the key messages you want to get across to the interviewer about yourself.
- Ensuring you have a good understanding of the company and the job you have applied for.
- Ensuring you are able to answer questions in a confident and concise manner and avoiding any 'blank moments' when you can't think of anything to say.

Preparing for an interview

Identified below are some of the key actions that you can do to prepare effectively for your interview.

Think about what they will want to find out from you:
- Try to see the situation from the interviewers' point of view – what will they want to find out about candidates for their vacancy in order to make the right selection decision?
- Identify the aspects the interviewers may want to assess using the information you have about the company and the role from the job advert, website or interview invitation. Highlight the key skills, qualities and knowledge that are important.
- Assess your own skills, qualities and knowledge against what they are looking for and identify your strengths and any development needs (see page 96).
- Prepare some examples of situations you have been in or things you have experienced that illustrate your strengths.

Think about the key messages you want to get over in the interview that describe your skills and qualities. In addition to what the interviewers may want to ask you, there may be information you want share to with them – the interview, after all, is your opportunity to sell yourself. While it is important not to dominate the conversation, there will be ways in which you can include this important information in the answers you provide. Information you may want to share with the interviewers may include the ideas listed opposite.

- Your commitment to this industry, type of work or company.
- Your enthusiasm for the role.
- The aspects of your skills, qualities and knowledge that you think set you aside from others.
- Any interest you have in developing further within their company.
- How you can contribute and add value to their organisation.

Make notes:

Make notes as you do your preparation; this will give you something quick and easy to refer to before you go into the interview and help focus your mind.

Many interviewers are happy for you to refer to notes as a memory jogger during the interview, but it is important to check that this is all right with them. Either ask when you go into the interview or call up beforehand and see if this is permitted. If you do take notes into the interview, remember the following important points:

- Make bullet point notes only because you will find that long-hand notes are hard to refer to quickly.
- Avoid reading your notes out verbatim – this will sound unnatural to the interviewer and not create the best impression.
- Focus on answering the question they have asked. It is easy to fall into the trap of using the examples/information you have prepared rather than actually answering the question they have asked.
- Accept you won't refer to all the information you have prepared.
- You may never refer to your notes, but they are there if you get nervous or flustered and need something to look at and focus your mind.

Re-read your CV:

Refresh your memory on answers you gave in your application form or information in your CV. The interviewers will probably have your application form or CV in front of them and are bound to ask some questions that refer to these documents. Just imagine how awful it would feel to be asked to elaborate on a situation you referred to in your application and have no memory of what you put and what they are referring to. You don't need that kind of anxiety in the interview, so have a look back through the information you submitted – you may even be able to take copies in with you to refer to if needed.

> **To impress an interviewer, do your company research. The question that foxed BT's graduate candidates this year was, 'What is our current share price?'**
> BT

Think of the worst question you could be asked:
What's the question you dread most? Assume they will ask you this. There is always a question we don't want to be asked in an interview because we don't know how to answer it. You can be sure that this is exactly one of the questions they will ask you, so be prepared and using this book make some notes on how you would answer it to show yourself in the best light.

Practise your answers:
You may think you are well prepared and have thought about how you would answer questions, but have you tried saying the answers out loud? Often people know what they want to say, but when they start speaking it comes out in a jumbled and unstructured manner.

A great way of overcoming this is to practise answering some questions. Ask a friend, colleague, family member or partner to ask you some questions and give you feedback on how the answers came across. While this kind of role play may seem a little embarrassing, it can be invaluable preparation. If you find the thought of doing this too much or don't have anyone to ask, then even just saying the answers out loud will help you assess whether or not they make sense.

Do some company research:
A key part of preparing for an interview is to do some background research into the company and the job. Doing this will enable you to:

● Make a proper assessment of whether it is the right job for you.
● Relate your skills and experience directly to the vacancy they are looking to fill.
● Sound knowledgeable in answering questions about the company and the advertised job.

Information you should find out

There is information about the company and the job that all candidates should research before attending an interview. This includes:

● Who the company are, what they do, where they are based and how many employees they have.
● What the job is about – its key activities or responsibilities.
● Any recent publicity or media content there has been about the company and its products or services.

TOP TIPS

When researching further information:

- Find out information relevant to the role/department you have applied for rather than focusing purely upon general company information.
- Find out about their company values or way of working. It is important for you to know if this really is the type, culture or style of organisation you want to be part of. For example, are they focused on team working when you prefer to work alone, or hard selling when you prefer to build long-term relationships with customers?
- If you are applying to a small local company, do some local research. Ask people what they know about the company and find out how well they are performing (see below) – the organisation is not likely to tell you if they are struggling financially.

Anything over and above that will really depend on the nature and seniority of the role you have applied for. For example, if you have applied for a marketing role the interviewer would expect you to have some knowledge of their products and services, marketing strategy and brand image. Likewise if you are applying for a senior role you should ensure that you have a good understanding of the organisation's performance results, strategy and the challenges that it currently faces.

Where you can find all this information

In the age of technology that we live in, accessing information about an organisation and their vacancies is easier then ever. Good sources of information include:

- Search the web using a search engine and the company name.
- Company website – this will have general information about the organisation and usually include a section on careers.
- Request a copy of the latest report and accounts.
- Review the original job advertisement and any information the company have sent you.
- Look in the local library for information.

If you have any additional questions about a company, don't be afraid of calling up and asking them prior to interview. You could speak with the interviewer, receptionist or Human Resources. If their premises are open to the public, then visit; if not, then try calling up and acting as a customer and seeing how well you are dealt with or how informative the conversation is.

Body language

As the saying goes, 'You never get a second chance to make a first impression,' the way you conduct yourself in terms of your body language is the most impactful way you communicate. This can range from your facial expressions to the way you stand or position yourself when sitting.

Making the most of your body language

It is important that you ensure your body language, voice tone and the words you are using are all giving the same message.

Do:

- Give a firm handshake – there is nothing worse than a 'wet lettuce' action.
- When you shake someone's hand say 'Hello' and their name (this will give you a better chance of remembering it or, even worse, using the wrong name) and look them in the eye.
- Maintain eye contact and keep your head up.
- Sit with an open, upright and attentive posture. You will appear interested and confident and will be able to breath properly and concentrate better.
- Be enthusiastic in your tone of voice.
- Smile and nod when appropriate.
- Place your hands in your lap, and use them for expression when needed.
- Have an active and confident walk – even when walking out of the building and to your car.
- Always accept water. Sip this to stop your mouth from drying up and it may give you time to think. It will also keep you hydrated and you will be able to concentrate better.

Don't:

- Cross your arms as this can make you appear defensive or aggressive.
- Fidget in your chair – you may appear nervous and uneasy.
- Lean your arms heavily on the table.

A perfect candidate is someone who is dressed appropriately for the role they have applied for, demonstrates an understanding of the organisation's values and aims, and shows real passion, enthusiasm and how they would add value.

SOPHIE MILLIKEN, MANAGER, RECRUITMENT, JOHN LEWIS

- Wave your hands around as you talk. This can become distracting and your interviewer may spend more time looking at your hands than listening to what you are saying.
- Fuss or fiddle with any papers you may have with you.
- Play with a pen.
- Accept a cup of tea or coffee if you are nervous.
- Flirt with the interviewer, even if he or she is flirting with you, this may be a set up.

Making the most of your appearance

We all have different interpretations of what is smart or casual dress – it is always best to play safe and err on the formal rather than informal. The clothes you wear can say a lot about you. You want the interviewer to be impressed but not distracted by what you are wearing. Sometimes people are not offered jobs because their appearance is inappropriate.

Do:
- Wear clothes that are comfortable.
- Clean your shoes, don't forget the heels.
- Wear shoes you can walk in with confidence.
- Wear clothes that don't crease too much.
- Wear something that reflects your personality.
- Make sure your hair is clean, brushed and tidy.
- Make sure you have washed beforehand.

Preparation

TOP TIPS

- If you know you get nervous and have hot sweaty palms, run your wrists under cold water.
- If you know your neck flushes, wear something that will cover this without making you excessively hot.
- If you are uncomfortable looking someone directly in the eyes, focus on the point between their eyes – they will never know the difference.
- If you can, visit the company at a time when people are starting or finishing work to see what people are wearing.
- Phone the company beforehand and ask if they have a dress code.
- If you are hot in an interview, ask if it is OK to remove your jacket or ask for the window to be opened. However, if you are prone to heavy sweating, you may be better sticking it out.
- If you are really unwell or reacting badly to medication, don't attend the interview and ask for another date if possible. The interviewer has to assess each candidate on what they see on the day so it will be difficult for them to make any allowances for you, because you are unwell, and still treat everyone fairly.

- Wear clothes that are appropriate for the job and organisation you are applying to. For instance, if you are being interviewed for a graphic designer, then the dress code is likely to be more casual. If you are being interviewed for a position in an office, then a formal suit will be more appropriate.

Don't:
- Wear too much aftershave or perfume, it may not be to everyone's liking.
- Wear clothes that are inappropriate for work.
- Wear too much make up.

What you should take into the interview

This all comes down to personal choice but here are some dos and don'ts:

Do:
- Take glasses if you use them, you may be asked to read something.
- Take a small bottle of water in case you aren't offered a drink.
- Take your CV, for clarification if needed.
- Take pen and paper, to make notes if you need to.
- Have a folder containing all of your paperwork.

Don't:
- Take in lots of papers or competitors' information. You might drop these or fiddle with them, which can become distracting.
- Take your shopping in with you – clothes or food.
- Take your children or your partner with you.

What you should do the night before an interview

There are a few suggestions to cope with night-before nerves. However, we are all different and you need to do what suits you.

Do:
- Have a good night's sleep.
- Refresh your mind with your prepared examples.
- Refresh your mind with what you would like to ask the interviewer.

Don't:
- Drink too much alcohol, the smell of this may linger into the next day.
- Eat strong flavoured food like garlic as this can be off-putting.
- Have a late night as you will need to be able to concentrate and focus.

2 Interview and interviewing styles

☑ Types of interview

☑ Interviewing styles

☑ Illegal and inappropriate questions

Types of interview

There are a variety of different types and styles of interviews that are conducted across all sectors of business and industry. In this section, we describe the most familiar ones.

....

Competency based interview

Competency based interviews work on the principle that the most accurate way of predicting future behaviour and performance is to understand how you have worked in the past. Interviewers assess this by asking individuals to provide real examples of situations they have been in.

There are no right and wrong answers to questions like these, the interviewer wants to understand your approach to situations you have encountered. During the interview you will be asked to choose and describe situations that demonstrate the competencies being assessed.

Chronological interview

These interviews look at your experience and career in date order. This approach is generally used at the beginning of the interview to get you talking and to put into context what you have done and why you have made the career choices you have. Consider the following:

- Talking through your education/career in date order.
- Describing your experiences within each of those positions.
- Keep it brief and avoid giving too much detail.
- Ask the interviewer if they would like you to expand.

CV-based interview

This approach is very similar to a chronological interview where the interviewer will ask you to talk through your CV, clarify your role, experiences and responsibilities within each position you have undertaken. However, this may not be in a chronological order. Be prepared for this and ensure you have your CV with you (see pages 94–100 for explaining any gaps in employment).

Portfolio interview

This is commonly used for more creative roles such as graphic designers, artists, interior designers or theatre stage design. This style of interview is likely to form part of the interview, so be prepared to talk through your experiences and skills in some detail. Portfolio information could include:

- Professional certificates.
- Research papers.
- Writing samples.
- Laboratory work.
- Examples of designs you have completed.
- Transcripts.

Telephone interview

Telephone interviews are becoming increasingly popular, particularly for organisations involved in high volume recruitment. They are used as a sifting method for assessment centres or a second round, face-to-face interview. Because you cannot make an impression in person it is important to create the right impression immediately on the phone. Telephone interviews generally last from 15 to 30 minutes.

Do:
- Sit down while you are on the phone, you may be inclined to walk about if you are standing and it is surprising how distracting this can be for the interviewer if your footsteps can be heard.
- Have your examples ready but try not to read from them.
- Be ready by the phone at the agreed time.
- Use a landline phone whenever you can; reception for mobiles and batteries running low can become a big frustration for both parties.

Don't:
- Be complacent because you can't be seen, it is still important to be prepared.
- Be in a location where you will get distracted.

Panel interview

A panel interview is more than simply one person asking questions. It is more usual these days for people to interview in pairs, particularly in larger organisations. The panel is likely to include the recruiting manager and a representative from Human Resources.

Panel interviews are very typical in the public sector, particularly within the Health Service, education and the Forces. These can be panels ranging from two to as many as five or six people. You should consider the points overleaf.

- Directing your answers to the whole panel.
- Ensuring you maintain eye contact with the whole panel of interviewers.
- Sitting yourself slightly back from the desk to enable you to have a better view of everyone and vary your eye contact.
- Ensuring you get each of their names, positions of responsibility and job title by asking them or, better still, by establishing this prior to the interview from Human Resources.

One-to-one interview
This is just one person conducting the interview and making the decision.

Internal interviews
These are never easy, especially if you know your interviewer fairly well. Try not to assume the interviewer knows everything about you and your achievements, you weren't born at your present company and you may have some good experiences you can draw on from previous roles, before you knew them. They are very likely to have set criteria for assessing you and if you miss out details of what you have done because you assume they know, you may well be leaving yourself short on evidence and hence be unsuccessful. Consider the following:

- Don't relax too much because you already know the interviewer, maintain professionalism throughout.
- Be prepared to answer some challenging questions relating to your peers (see page 46 for advice).

Interviewing styles

As well as different types of interview and interview questions, you will encounter a range of interviewers, in terms of experience and style, so be prepared to deal with all of these. This section explains more about these different types of question and how to handle those interviewers who are aggressive, inexperienced or nervous and those that like the sound of their voice more than listening to yours.

Hypothetical questions

The interviewer will describe a situation and ask you what would you do or what decision you would make if you were in that situation. You may also be given a number of options to choose from. Don't feel restricted by them and, if you wouldn't take any of them, then say so. For example, you could say, 'I would take A to a point, however, I would also do X and Y.'

Situational questions

Situations are set up that simulate common problems you may encounter on the job. Your responses and approach to these situations are assessed and measured against predetermined behavioural indicators. This approach is likely to be used as part of an interview only. The interviewer is keen to understand the approach or considerations you make in these types of situations.

Stress techniques

Stress techniques are sometimes used where the interviewer intentionally attempts to upset you to see how you react under pressure. You may be asked questions that make you uncomfortable, you may be interrupted when you are speaking, or have a series of questions fired at you very quickly. It is uncommon for an entire interview to be conducted under pressurised conditions, but if you are applying for a role that is going to be pressurised, the company is going to want to find out how you cope with stress in the workplace. Often interviewers will take on specific roles for the interview, for instance, the 'good cop/bad cop' scenario. Consider handling these situations in the ways that are described in the list overleaf.

Relax, let your personality show through and provide a range of examples to demonstrate the various competencies that the organisation recruits to.

SOPHIE MILLIKEN, MANAGER, RECRUITMENT, JOHN LEWIS

Interview and interviewing styles

- Remain calm.
- Take your time.
- Smile.
- Don't take it personally.
- Think about what they are asking and then respond concisely.
- Remember they are not necessarily like this on a day-to-day basis.

Incompetent interviewers

Unfortunately, there are a lot of people interviewing who have not been trained properly, are inexperienced or ask inappropriate questions (see pages 24–8) – and sometimes all three.

Some interviewers have poor technique and may well ask you a series of questions all at once leaving you feeling confused and wondering what the first question was that they asked you. Don't be afraid to ask them to break down the question, starting from the beginning again. Or say, 'Can I just clarify what you asked in the beginning.' Consider handling such interviewers using the following actions:

- Repeat the question back to ensure you have heard it correctly.
- Ask them to repeat the question.
- Make a note of the question as they ask it.

Nervous interviewers

Inexperienced interviewers will often be as, if not more, nervous than you. If they seem anxious and take a long time to ask follow-on questions, don't let it put you off, be patient with them and ensure that you work at their pace.

An inexperienced interviewer will often work alongside a colleague – don't dismiss their contribution to the meeting just because they haven't interviewed very often. The individual may well be a very good judge of people and actually be the person you would end up working for.

What not to do in an interview

As much as you may want to say, 'What a stupid question!' and, 'Why would you want to know that?', or, 'I don't know what you are talking about', keep your opinions to yourself and your emotions at bay. It would be a shame to do something inappropriate that could affect your chances of getting the job.

Don't:

- Refuse to answer a question – establish first why they are asking this of you and explain why you would prefer not to answer if that is how you feel.
- Take over the interview.
- Turn the interview into firing a round of questions back to them.
- Patronise the interviewer, who may know more than you think.
- Raise your voice.
- Ignore a member of the interview panel because you don't like them, they are not asking the questions or you don't think they are important.
- Direct all of your answers at one person.
- Become emotional or aggressive if you are being put under pressure.
- Get into an argument with your interviewer.

At Microsoft, the best candidates are people who will always ask questions, look for new solutions to old problems and challenge the status quo. Having the desire and ability to learn, adapt and explore the opportunities an organisation like ours offers is just as important as being top of your class or the best sales person in the country. It's important that we have the right people for the right job and if candidates demonstrate the talent and drive we need, then there may be a place for them at Microsoft.

THERESA MCHENRY, PEOPLE AND ORGANISATION CAPABILITY, MICROSOFT UK

Illegal and inappropriate questions

Discrimination on the basis of race, marital status, age, gender, colour, sexual orientation, religion, national origin, gender reassignment or disability is illegal. Questions that are discriminatory should be very few and far between. However, it is possible that you may be asked a question that is discriminatory, particularly by an inexperienced interviewer or someone who has little understanding of the employment law surrounding selection. The interviewer may or may not be aware that they are asking a question that could be perceived by a candidate as being discriminatory. There are a variety of ways in which you can respond to these types of questions.

You are quite justified to decline to answer the question. Politely say that you do not wish to answer such a question as you feel it is inappropriate and are unsure as to how it is relevant to the role you have applied for. For example, you could say, 'I am not sure how relevant this is to the position I have applied for and would prefer not to answer that question.'

Alternatively, you can respond to the question without referring to its inappropriateness or ignore the inappropriateness and focus on the concern that is behind the question. For example, say, 'I think what you are asking is...', or, 'Are you trying to establish if...', and select the answer you wish to give.

Whether or not you choose to answer the question, the concern that is likely to remain in your mind will be, 'Do I want to work in an environment that might subject me to such potentially discriminatory practices?'

If you feel you may have been discriminated against, contact the Commission for Equality and Human Rights (www.equalityhumanrights.com) or your local Citizens Advice Bureau (www.adviceguide.org.uk) for further advice. It is important that you take action promptly as there is a time limit on making a claim against discrimination. The following is a list of questions that could be regarded as illegal or inappropriate together with some suggested responses.

....

Are you planning to start a family?
- Are you asking if I am able to work overtime?
- Are you asking if I would have commitment to this position?

Are you married?
- I am not sure how relevant that is to the role, but if you are trying to establish if I am able to commit to working extra hours or overtime, then the answer is yes.

How many children do you have?

- Are you asking me if I will be able to commit to the flexible working hours outlined in the job description?
- Are you asking me if I can work additional hours when they are required to get a project finished?

You may have to travel a lot in this role. Will that be an issue for your family?

- Are you asking me if I am able to commit to travelling and being away from my family?

How will you cope with childcare arrangements if you were offered this position?

- Are you asking if I can be relied upon to be punctual and work additional hours if required?

Are you pregnant?

- I am not sure why you are asking this question?

How old are you?

- Are you asking how many years of experience I have?
- Are you asking how many more years I have left to work?

How many more years do you see yourself working for?

- Are you wanting to know how if I can be relied upon to work for the next five years?
- Are you asking me if I am near retirement age?

What religion are you?

- Are you asking me if I require specific requirements to suit my religion?
- Are you asking me if I am able to adapt to the working environment because of my religion?

What country were you born in?

● Are you trying to establish whether or not I have the right to be working in the UK?

Where do your parents come from?

● Are you trying to establish my nationality?

How long have you lived in this country?

● Are you trying to establish my nationality?
● Are you trying to establish how fluent my English is?
● Are you trying to establish how familiar I am with working practices in the UK?

What nationality are you?

● Why do you ask?
● Is this for monitoring purposes for equal opportunities?
● Are you asking if I have the right to work in the UK?

Have you ever filed for bankruptcy?

● I am not sure of the relevance of this question as this role has no financial responsibility.

Have you ever been arrested?

● If you are asking if I have any unspent criminal convictions, then, no, I don't.

How do you deal with your disability on a day-to-day basis at work?

● I am not sure what you are trying to get at with this question, but I am happy to describe the reasonable adjustments I would require in the workplace if I were offered the job.

What sexual orientation are you?

● I am not sure what relevance that has?

Do you have any health issues?

- Are you trying to ascertain if I have any form of disability that I would like to declare?

I see you have a disability, how do you think that will affect how you do your job?

- I am not sure what you are trying to get at with this question, but I am happy to describe the reasonable adjustments I would require in the workplace if I were offered the job.

Do you drink alcohol or use recreational drugs?

- I am not sure of the relevance of this question to this role. However, I can assure you that I do not believe it is appropriate to go to work under the influence of alcohol or drugs.

What political party do you support?

- I am not sure why you are asking that question, but I prefer to keep my political beliefs between myself and the ballot box.

Are you a member of a trade union?

- I am not sure why you are asking me that particular question, but I believe this is a personal matter that each individual has the right to make a choice about.

How many years has it been since you graduated from college/ university?

- Why do you ask?
- Are you interested in how old I am?

Some colleagues you will be working with are much older/ younger than you, is that a problem?

- I enjoy working with all sorts of people.

How do you plan on getting to work?

- I am not sure if you are asking this as you are concerned about my punctuality for work, but I can assure you that I have a good punctuality and attendance record.

You will be working with all an all-male/female team, is that a problem to you?

- Are you asking me if I have a problem working with people who are the opposite sex to myself?

3 Qualifications and work experience

....

☑ **Explaining your qualifications**

☑ **Relevant experiences at work**

☑ **If you are over- or under qualified**

☑ **Internal posts**

Explaining your qualifications

The focus of this section is to give you guidance on how to answer the many questions you are likely to face about your qualifications and experience. Providing interviewers with strong answers to these questions is particularly important – they want to assess your experience in some detail and decide whether or not you are up to the job. It's all very well reading about you in your CV or application form but now they want to hear it from you!

Describe your experience to date and how you believe it relates to this role?

The interviewer needs you to focus on your experience that is relevant to the particular role you are being interviewed for – avoid the temptation to go back to the point where you left school and talk through every job you have ever had. Instead, in your answer include:

- A brief summary of your previous experience that relates to the role.
- A more in-depth description of your current/most recent role and how it relates to the role you are being interviewed for.
- Highlight the relevant skills and knowledge that you have developed that will benefit you in this role.

Avoid:

- Talking for 15 minutes around this one area – the interviewer will have lots more questions to ask you.
- Getting muddled up about the sequence of jobs you have had. The interviewer will have your CV/application in front of him or her – ensure that you do too.
- Talking at length about a position you had that bears no relevance to the job you are being interviewed for.

If applying to a job advert, ensure your covering letter plays back the key candidate criteria that are being looked for – and use examples.

ROB VOSS, DIRECTOR OF HUMAN RESOURCES UK, SIEMENS FINANCIAL SERVICES

Example

I have had a variety of roles in the service sector over the years and have worked my way up from front line roles such as being a waiter, receptionist and shop assistant into ones with more responsibility for leading a team. My current role is probably the most relevant as it has allowed me to develop a good blend of management and service improvement skills that I think would be particularly useful in the vacancy that you are looking to fill.

What experiences from previous roles can you bring to this role?

Differing a little from the question to the left, the interviewer wants you to identify some specific experiences that you believe are relevant to this role rather than give a full summary of your career. Experiences that could be considered as relevant are:

- When you have had a role with similar responsibilities.
- When you have carried out some of the tasks that you would be doing in this role.
- Any training or qualifications you have that are directly relevant to this position.

> ### REMEMBER!
>
> *In your answer demonstrate that you understand what the role is about by focusing on experiences that are directly relevant to the key tasks or responsibilities of the role – two or three will be sufficient.*

Example

My previous job had similar responsibilities – carrying out market research with members of the public and analysing the data and producing recommendations for our clients. It was in a different market but the skills I developed would be useful in this job. I have also learnt how to get the best from groups of people so would be pretty much able to hit the ground running.

What are the reasons for your success in your career to date?

Reason for success can be varied, but may include:

- Sheer hard work.
- Lucky breaks along the way.
- Proactively managing your career.
- Making sacrifices in your personal life to achieve at work.
- Support of other people at work – a mentor or manager.
- Dedication and a drive to succeed.

The interviewer wants to find out how you operate and the approach you are likely to take to succeeding in this role. In your answer:

- Describe the key reasons for your success.
- Indicate what you have learnt from achieving success in this way.

Avoid:

- Suggesting that it was all just luck.
- Indicate it's because you are so fantastic at your job, you were bound to succeed – no one likes a big head.
- Alluding to the fact that a relative or friend gave you your lucky breaks.

Qualifications and work experience

Example

I think there are two key reasons for the success I have had in my career to date – the first was a manager who gave me valuable guidance and opportunities. In addition to that, I have always worked hard and sought opportunities to learn new skills and apply these whenever possible.

What are the reasons for any shortcomings in your career to date?

If there are lessons you have learnt or changes you have made to how you approach your working life, then talk to the interviewer about them. Recognising shortcomings in your approach to your career and being able to describe the actions you have taken to address these will demonstrate maturity on your part and will be viewed positively by the interviewer. In your answer:

Do:
- Identify any shortcomings in your career to date.
- Indicate what actions you have taken to overcome these shortcomings.
- Describe what you have learnt from these.

Don't:
- Place the blame entirely upon other people or circumstances – take personal responsibility.
- Be negative or appear hard done by.

Example

I think I would have made better progress in my career if I had taken it more seriously earlier on. To begin with, a job was just a way of earning money to go out with my friends and to travel. After a few years I realised I needed to take it more seriously – all my colleagues were progressing and I wasn't. I put more effort into developing myself and achieving at work and soon reaped the benefits. Looking back on it I'm really glad I did this.

What training have you completed?

Focus the main part of your answer on describing training you have done that is relevant to the role you have applied for before mentioning briefly any other significant training you have completed. In your answer:

Do:
- State the key training courses.
- Indicate what skills or knowledge you developed by completing the courses.
- Indicate how you have used these skills or this knowledge.
- Describe how this will be useful for the job you have applied for.

Don't:
- Go through every course you have ever done.
- Spend a lot of time talking about irrelevant courses.
- Mention those you would like to take as this does not address the question.
- Give lots of excuses as to why you haven't been on any courses.

Example

I have done quite a few courses with my current employer, including one on effective team working and another on team leadership. I learnt a lot about how to get the best out of others by adapting my style to suit the needs of the individuals, which would benefit me in this role.

What qualifications do you have that would be relevant to this job?

Begin your answer by describing any qualifications you have that are essential for the job, such as a financial planning certificate for the role of financial adviser, and then go on to indicate any other relevant ones. Indicate the key learning points from doing these qualifications and why you did them.

Example

I have completed all the relevant customer service NVQs and have found these helpful in being better at understanding how best to organise myself. The fact that I have done these indicates to employers that I am serious about a career in this sector and I am able to offer help and support to others.

> **TOP TIP**
>
> Don't feel you need to go into details about what exam results you got – if this is important to the interviewer they will ask.

Describe your IT skills

Give a brief overview of the programmes you are familiar with and the level at which you can operate. Most users are familiar with the terms basic, intermediate and advanced to describe levels of competence. If you are currently developing any new IT skills, then indicate what these are and what courses you are completing. Answers could include:

- I use Word, Excel and PowerPoint on a regular basis and would describe myself as an intermediate level user on each of these.
- I use Word a lot and am currently attending courses to improve my Excel skills as this is something that is now required in my work.

Avoid:
- Overstating your expertise. You will only be found out if they ask you to do a quick practical test or once you have got the job.

Relevant experiences at work

It is important to ensure you are able to explain your relevant experience to the interviewer and how these experiences relate to the job you are applying for. This will be particularly important should you be in a position where your qualifications are not at the required level for the job.

In what ways are you better at your job than your colleagues?

Rather than focusing on what some of your colleagues aren't so good at and comparing yourself to that, talk about what you are particularly good at. Pick just a couple of things rather than relating a long list of activities that you are wonderful at. Indicate in your answer:

- The areas of work you feel you are particularly strong at.
- Why you think you are good at these tasks.
- How you helped your colleagues develop similar skills.

Avoid:
- Complaining how useless some of your colleagues are – it isn't professional to do this and you never know, they may be acquainted with the person you are describing.

Example

I have quite a lot of experience using Excel spreadsheets to analyse data, so this is something the team seem to look to me to do for them. These skills are particularly useful at month end when we get everyone's figures in and have to turn them into something meaningful for the directors. I have recently started taking some of the other team members through what I do and gradually building their confidence in using Excel.

In what ways are you worse at your job than your colleagues? What could you do better?

We are all good at different things at work; there is nothing wrong with not being the best at something in the team. In your answer:

Do:
- Identify clearly what it is that you are not as good at doing as others.
- Indicate what you have done, or are doing, to remedy this.
- Briefly describe what you are good at that may compensate for your shortcomings.

Don't:

- Pick something that is critical to the role.
- Indicate that you have taken little action to develop, that's just what you are like.
- Indicate that you can't think of anything as you can undertake all tasks.

Example

I think everyone in the team would recognise that I am not the best person at completing paperwork accurately. I am, however, good with the customers and always way ahead of the others on sales. To try to improve my paperwork skills I have asked one of the supervisors to check what I have done and give me feedback on what needs to be changed.

What are the key tasks in your role?

The interviewer wants to assess whether or not you understand the priorities in your existing role and why these tasks are important for the organisation. In your answer:

Do:

- State clearly the tasks you believe are a priority in your role.
- Indicate why they are important; for example, they contribute to meeting targets.
- Briefly describe how you complete these tasks, the actions you take.

Don't:

- Describe everything that you do – limit yourself to five or six tasks.
- State you don't know why they are important tasks for the organisation, you are just asked to do them before anything else.

Example

The key tasks in my role are to ensure that all the reports that go out are accurate, well presented and on time. To do this I keep a constant check on deadlines and liaise with my colleagues to ensure they have prepared them with time to spare. I then check through all the information in the reports for accuracy and that it tallies with the database. These tasks are important because they link to some of our performance targets and the organisation receives funding based upon how well we meet those targets.

Describe a typical day in your current job.

A good way to help the interviewer understand the key activities in your job and, more importantly, how you approach them is to talk him or her through

Qualifications and work experience

a typical day. Try to highlight the skills and qualities that you know the interviewer is looking for. For example, if you have already been asked a lot of questions about prioritising work and being efficient, then indicate how you do this in a typical day. Spend some time familiarising yourself with the job description as this can give you a good steer as to what the interviewer is looking for. In your answer:

- Give a brief overview of the sequence of the key events in a typical day.
- Focus more attention on the priority areas.
- Describe the typical challenges that you face in a day and how you like to deal with them.

Avoid:
- Going into minute detail about every task that you complete.
- Describe a day that has no challenges in it.

Example

A typical day will begin with completing any tasks that were left over from the day before. I then check the diary system and identify any deadlines that are coming up that I need to work to. I liaise with my colleagues to prioritise the tasks for the team as a whole and we agree who is going to do what. Although we always try to plan our activities, you have to be prepared for someone coming to you with a last-minute request for a report. I ensure I stagger my lunch breaks and check there is always cover in the office for phone calls or visitors. In this way, I make sure we stay on top of tasks and can achieve our deadlines and service level agreements.

Why should we give you this job?

One of the hardest questions you can be asked – there is really no right answer! You need to convince the interviewer that you are the right person for the job and no one else will do, and all without sounding insincere. Consider including the following in your answer:

- The skills you have that make you right for the job.
- The qualities you have that mean you would be great at the job.
- Your commitment and enthusiasm for the role.
- Any longer-term career aims you may have that would fit with the organisation.

Example

Because I am the best person for it! I have a genuine enthusiasm for the work that you do here and can bring lots of relevant experience from my last job. I have excellent interpersonal skills and a track record of delivering results. From what you have described, it also seems important to you that you have people in the company who are prepared to take on a challenge and that is certainly me!

We would like to follow up your references before taking things any further. Is that OK?

You want to say yes because you know they will be good and you are keen to get the job. One problem may be that your potential employer insists that one referee has to be from your current employer and, of course, they don't know you are looking for another job.

Don't be afraid of standing your ground and insisting that the interviewer must not approach your current employer before you have received and accepted the job offer. This is standard practice. The interviewer wouldn't like it if the first they knew about a member of their own staff leaving was a reference request.

> **REMEMBER!**
>
> *In some sectors, such as in education, it is standard practice to request a reference prior to interview.*

Example

I am really pleased that you want to progress my application further and am happy for you to approach any of my referees except my current employer. Although I have no doubts that their reference will be glowing, I am sure you can appreciate that you approaching them could jeopardise my position with them as they are not aware I am job hunting at the moment. Obviously, if I had accepted a formal job offer from you and told them I was leaving, then that would be fine. I hope you can understand my position on this.

Why are you looking to move on from your current role?

There is nothing wrong with wanting to find a new job, but it is important that you give a convincing reason for wanting to move on, and even better if you can link that reason to their particular vacancy. For example, if the job offers the potential to develop new skills, then indicating this is one of your reasons for moving on will be seen as positive. In your answer:

● Identify clearly why you are job hunting.
● Describe how this role will fulfil what you want from a new role.
● Remain positive and upbeat about your current role and employer.

Avoid:
● Dwelling on the negative aspects of your current role or employer.

Qualifications and work experience

- Indicating you are not too bothered, you are just having a look around at the marketplace – they will see you as a time waster.
- Appearing desperate to move on.

Example

I am looking to move on from my current job as I am keen to continue to develop my skills and broaden my experience of the industry. Unfortunately, this isn't possible with my current employer as it is only a small company. I am attracted to this role as I think it will give me a wider experience and a fresh challenge. It is particularly interesting because of the new product areas you have recently gone into.

Why should we give this role to an external person rather than promote someone from inside the company?

By asking this, the interviewer is probably seeing how well you stand up to a challenging question – if they weren't seriously considering external as well as internal candidates, you probably wouldn't have been invited for an interview. Focus your answer on selling the benefits of yourself as an external candidate, these may include:

- Bringing fresh ideas in from another company or competitor.
- You have no history with the company, so have no issues about changes that may be happening at the moment.
- You have experience of doing a similar role in a different company or environment, so maybe able to spot improvements that could be made more easily than existing staff.
- You have worked for a competitor, so are well placed to know how to compete successfully against them.
- It is good to bring a new person into the team occasionally otherwise people can get set in their ways.

TOP TIP

Avoid directly, or indirectly, criticising internal applicants for the role.

If you are over- or under qualified

This section looks at particularly challenging questions that you may be asked if you are over- or under qualified for a role. The interviewers' suspicions may be aroused and they will want to explore their concerns in some detail with you.

Why are you applying for a job for which you appear to be overqualified?

Your reasons may include:

- You want to take a step back in responsibilities and do a job that you really enjoy rather than a more senior one.
- You want to take a step back in responsibilities in order to achieve a better work/life balance due to family commitments.
- You want to move into a different area/function and feel the best way to do this is by starting in a more junior role.
- Since being made redundant you are finding it difficult to secure a job at the same level as your last one – you are keen to stay in work so have applied for a more junior position.

Avoid:
- Indicating that you see it as a stop gap until something better comes along.
- Suggesting that times are hard and that you are only doing this to earn some money.
- Appearing disinterested in the role.
- Indicating that you see the role as beneath you and will be looking for promotion quickly.

> **Think deeply about how you have distinguished yourself from your peers. Highlight where you have over- achieved and showcase areas you have a real passion for.**
>
> IAN SHARP, ENGINEERING RECRUITER, GOOGLE UK

How do we know that you won't get bored and want to move on quickly?

This is an obvious concern for an employer if you have had a more senior or challenging role previously. You can overcome this by:

- Explaining the reasons you have applied for the role.
- Identifying the aspects of the role that you would find enjoyable or rewarding and explaining why you feel that way.

- Indicate what your longer-term aims are and how this role fits in with them.
- Indicating that you do not consider the role to be a boring one.

Example

I have applied for the role as it means less travelling than my current position and I think this will give me a better work/life balance. However, I certainly haven't just applied for anything, I have thought carefully about what skills I have and the things I enjoy doing. I think this role would be very interesting and would provide me with the opportunity of working in a new sector. I would like to become part of an organisation locally that I could enjoy being part of and stay with for some time and your company seems like my kind of place.

Having run your own business what has led you to apply for a job now?

Your reasons for leaving self-employment may include:

- You miss corporate life.
- You miss working in a team.
- You find it difficult to balance work and home life running your own business and would like to return to the more structured environment of employment.
- You have given it your best shot but are not achieving the results you would like to due to the current environment or nature of the business you were running.
- You need and have missed the motivation and inspiration from working with others.

Do:
- State clearly why you are job hunting.
- Describe what you have learnt from being self-employed.
- Relate this learning to the role you have applied for.

Don't:
- Sound desperate, saying, for example, that it has all been a huge financial disaster for you.
- Describe how fantastically successful you have been – this will only heighten the interviewer's concerns about your motivation for the job.

Example

I have really enjoyed the last few years running my own business, but miss the daily interaction with a team of people and the opportunity to see things through in the long term. Working as a consultant has been a great way of gaining exposure to lots of different organisations, but I sometimes feel frustrated that I am often not there to see things through to the end or the results of my hard work.

How will you cope with being managed by someone who is less qualified or experienced than yourself?

You need to indicate that although you may be more experienced or well qualified than the manager that you will give him or her your full support and co-operation and not undermine the manager's authority. You may also want to suggest that you may be able to assist with some tasks, if appropriate, and take some of the load.

Example
Although I may have had several years of management experience and a qualification in this I would never pretend to know everything. We all have different ways of doing things and I would respect their judgement – I am sure they wouldn't be in the role if they weren't capable of doing it. I would, of course, be happy to offer help on tasks if they felt that was appropriate. I am really just looking forward to being part of a team rather than having the responsibility of managing other people.

You have run your own business and been your own boss. How will you feel about being managed by someone?

The interviewer wants to be reassured that this won't be an issue for you. Indicate how you feel about it and say why you feel that way. Your answers could include:

- I have done project work in my clients' businesses so have been used to being managed.
- Managing other people and running a business has given me a better appreciation of the challenges of these responsibilities.
- I am really much more of a team member than I am a leader, so it shouldn't be a problem.
- I am not at all worried about this, it will be nice to have someone to work with and discuss things with.
- I am sure I will be able to learn a lot from them.

Avoid:
- Indicating that you are a bit of an independent spirit and will find being managed by someone difficult.

Qualifications and work experience

- Quizzing the interviewer about the management style of the individual and how closely you will be supervised.
- Stating, 'I am sure I can give some advice and pointers.'

What concerns do you have about taking on a role at this more junior level?

Seek to reassure the interviewer that you have thought this move through, but don't just brush the question off with an unconsidered, 'I don't have any concerns.' Concerns you have may be more about the perceptions of others rather than any personal concerns – if this is the case, indicate how you will address these.

Example

I have thought carefully about this move and believe it is the right thing for me. However, I am aware that others may have concerns about my motivations for the role and think I may not stick it out. To overcome these I would demonstrate my commitment by working hard, becoming involved in the team and organisation and showing what additional things I could contribute because of my previous experience that may benefit the team as a whole.

You have been working at a much more junior level up to now, why are you interested in applying for this role?

The interviewer clearly has some concerns about the appropriateness of your application to have asked such a question, so you need to convince him or her that you have the skills and qualities required, even if you are not the most obvious candidate. In your answer:

- Acknowledge the interviewer's concern – you can see it may look like a big jump.
- Explain clearly why you think you have the right skills and qualities.
- Give an example, if possible, of when you have had similar responsibilities or use an example from outside the workplace.
- Emphasise that you are looking for a challenging role, you would like to be stretched further.

Avoid:

- Suggesting that you just thought you would try applying – it's good practice having an interview. You will be seen as a time waster.
- Indicating you don't know what the interviewer means, you are more than ready for this role.

Example

I feel that I have developed many of the skills needed in this role and am looking for a challenging next move. I am not really stretched in my current job so thought it was important to move on and develop my career further. I can see it looks like I am making a big jump, but I have often deputised for my manager when she has been away and so have some experience of carrying out similar responsibilities.

Why are you trying to leap a couple of stages in your career progression?

You need to give the interviewer some clear rationale for wanting to take a different career progression route than would normally be expected. Reasons might include:

- You are ambitious and have ensured that you have developed quickly in your current role.
- You have had feedback to suggest that you are capable of the role you have applied for.
- You like a challenge and are prepared to work hard.
- You are more focused on finding a job that is right for you and that you could perform well in, rather than following the more normal career development route.

Example

I am looking to take a big step up in responsibilities at this stage as I enjoy a challenge at work and have worked really hard preparing myself for such a position. As well as taking every opportunity at work I have also done some study in my own time that I think would stand me in good stead in this role.

What concerns do you have about applying for this more senior role?

Without appearing too doubtful about taking on such a role it is good to acknowledge that you recognise that it will be challenging for you. Other concerns may be how other people may regard your application – you know that they may feel you are being over ambitious. If this is the case, then seek to reassure the interviewer that you are the right person for the job.

Avoid:

- Dismissing the question with, 'I don't have any.' You will demonstrate a more mature approach to the job by acknowledging its challenges.

Example

I am obviously aware that it will be a big step up in responsibility for me and I will face some challenges. However, my only real concerns are more about how other people perceive my application. I am concerned that they will assume it is too much of a jump for me to make and not give me the chance to prove myself. I hope through this selection process that I am able to demonstrate that I have the necessary skills and qualities and how committed I am to securing this position and succeeding in it.

What challenges do you think you would face if you were successful in securing this more senior role?

Acknowledge the challenges you think you will face – this isn't a sign of any weaknesses. Indicate how you will tackle these challenges and what you will learn from them.

Avoid:
- Identifying a long list of challenges – focus upon two or three key ones.
- Indicating you are not sure how you would tackle them.
- Denying you will face any challenges – this is unrealistic and will be viewed as such by the interviewer.

Example

I think the most challenging aspects of the role for me will be getting to know and understand such a big team quickly so that I can support them effectively, and getting to grips with what my role is in the management team. To address these I will prioritise spending time with the team on a one-to-one basis and as a group and ask my line manager to give me some guidance on what my colleagues expect of me.

Internal posts

A lot of the questions you will be asked when applying for a role with your current employer will be exactly the same as if you were an external applicant and on pages 18–28 you will find some guidance on how best to approach this type of interview.

There are also, however, likely to be some questions specific to you as an internal applicant exploring how you will manage relationships with colleagues if you are successful, or deal with the disappointment if you are unsuccessful.

How do you think your colleagues will react should you be appointed in this role?

Include in your answer an honest assessment of how you think they will react. If you feel there are some who will be pleased for you and others that will find it more difficult, then say so. The interviewer is probably aware of the characters involved and will have his or her own views on any issues you may face if appointed. In your answer identify:

- The positive reactions you think you will get.
- Any negative reactions you think you may get.
- How you will manage those negative reactions.

Example
I think most of the team will be genuinely very pleased for me but there are a couple who may be a bit jealous and think it should have been them. I would work hard to demonstrate that I was the right person for the job by being good at what I do. I would also seek to involve any colleagues who still had reservations in what I was doing and ensure they feel they are valued members of the team.

How will you approach working with your colleagues if you are successful in securing this new role?

When taking up a new position in a team, maybe a promotion or more specialist role, you may not only encounter concern or jealousy from colleagues who would have liked the job, but your day-to-day working relationships with them may have changed. Instead of doing the same job as some of them you may now have different responsibilities. Make it clear to the interviewer how you would tackle this – see overleaf.

- Manage this change of relationship.
- Ensure that you focus on your new responsibilities rather than being dragged back into what you used to do.
- Help your colleagues to understand your new responsibilities and what you will need from them.

Example

I would take some time to understand the role a little more and then I think it would be good to explain to my colleagues what my new job is all about and that although I would still be sitting with them, I would be focusing on quite different tasks. I would also explain clearly the data that I needed from them and the timescales that we need to meet. I would also see if they thought there was any support they needed from me in my new capacity.

How will you approach managing people who used to be your peers?

The interviewer will be aware of the challenges that many people face when managing people they used to work alongside and will want to assess whether or not you understand these potential issues and if you have a strategy for managing them. Potential issues might include:

- Staff being upset they didn't get the job themselves.
- Concern that you know too much about them and may use this to your advantage when managing them, such as an inability to always pull their weight in the team.
- Lack of respect for you as a manager when the day before you were just one of them.

Approaches to overcoming these issues might be:

- Acknowledging their concerns up front and indicating how you will manage these.
- Encouraging those who feel positive about your promotion to share why they feel like this with their colleagues.
- Keeping a regular dialogue going with individuals with concerns so that issues don't grow out of control.
- Challenging any negative behaviour that you come across in a firm but empathetic manner.

Example

I already know there are a couple of people who will think it is strange that I have suddenly become their manager after working with them all these years. I would manage these concerns by meeting the team as a whole and indicating how I intend to approach managing them. I would also have regular one-to-one meetings and monitor, as part of those, our relationship and any issues they may have with me. I would treat all the team fairly but firmly and try to adapt my approach to meet their individual needs.

Your previous performance reviews have not always been satisfactory. How can we be sure you will perform well in this role?

One of the drawbacks of being an internal candidate is the interviewers know a lot about you. Acknowledge their concerns and describe the improvements you have made since this happened. You may even be able to offer an explanation for the poor reviews.

Example

In 2007 I had two poor performance reviews. I was going through a bad patch at home and stupidly I let it affect my performance at work. Once I had eventually explained what was going on, my manager was really encouraging and supportive and helped me to see the importance of being able to separate work from your personal life. I learnt a lot from this situation and have been able to apply myself at work in a much more focused way since. This has led to me having good and excellent ratings in my performance reviews over the last 18 months.

> **TOP TIP**
>
> Concentrate your answer on reassuring the interviewer that you have learnt from the poor performance reviews you had and do not intend to let it happen again.

You had relationship issues with your previous manager, why was this?

Indicate in your answer:

- What the relationship issues were.
- Why you think they occurred.
- What you did to try to improve the situation.
- What you learnt from this situation.

> **REMEMBER!**
>
> *Don't place the blame entirely on the other person, even if you did find him or her impossible. Indicate that you recognise the need to take some responsibility yourself for what happened.*

Example

I think we got off to a bad start as I got a bit caught up in disciplinary action that was being taken against one of my colleagues. I was their union representative in the official meeting and, of course, that was my first real encounter with my new manager. I felt he had a bit of a problem with me being such an active union member and we continually seemed to be disagreeing on things in the office. I know I can be a bit 'full on' for some people, always speaking my mind, so I decided to try to do something to improve our relationship. I asked if I could spend some time at our next one-to-one meeting explaining why I do my union work and what it involves. He seemed to find this quite interesting and things were a little easier after that.

How will you feel if you don't get this promotion?

The interviewer wants to know how you will handle the disappointment if you don't get offered the job. In your answer:

Do:
- Acknowledge you will be disappointed.
- Indicate that you will ask for feedback on what you could have done better so you are ready for the next opportunity that comes along.
- Reassure the interviewer that you will not let it affect your performance in your job and that you remain committed to the company.

Don't:
- Indicate that you will be angry and upset.
- Indicate that if you don't get it this time, you will probably give up and look elsewhere for a job.
- Quiz them as to whether they are trying to let you down gently by asking this in the interview.

Example
Obviously I will be disappointed if I don't get offered the job, but I will use this selection process as an opportunity to learn and ask for feedback in what I could have done better at interview and identify any skills I need to develop. By doing this I will be in a much better position next time a vacancy comes up. I won't let my disappointment affect my relationship with whoever does get the job and will offer them my full support.

4 Getting your foot in the door

- ☑ Questions for school leavers
- ☑ Questions for graduates
- ☑ For school leavers and graduates

Questions for school leavers

With little or no work experience, it can be hard to convince an interviewer that you are the right person for the job, worth the investment and the potential risk. Unlike other candidates, you have limited work history to draw upon so it is important that you are able to describe your skills, qualities and experiences as clearly as possible. These could be from clubs, societies, sports teams or part-time jobs. It is important also to demonstrate your willingness and desire to learn from others, develop further and to work hard.

What was your favourite subject?

This question is generally asked to get you talking and to make you feel more comfortable in the interview. It can describe a lot about you in terms of your preferred interest areas and how you take in information. Are you someone who enjoys the right/wrong of mathematics and analysing problems or do you enjoy topics that require more research and debate? Or maybe you are the kind of person who would have done anything to get outside onto the sports playing field. It is important to:

● State the subject you enjoyed and why.
● Indicate what you got out of this – the skills you obtained.

Example

I really enjoyed sociology. I found it fascinating learning about the differing opinions and cultures of the world. I particularly enjoyed the interaction and debating with others as I feel I learn more from talking about things rather than having to read lots of information. However, I have to say that I also really enjoyed the team spirit you get from the active sports side of physical education.

> **TOP TIP**
>
> To help you to describe some of the key skills that you have or that you've developed in the work place, refer to the descriptive words on page 246.

Which subjects were you best at?

This may be clear from the results you obtained. It is worth explaining why you think you are good at these subjects and if they tie in with subjects you enjoyed. It may well be that you have a natural ability to learn languages, but you didn't really enjoy them.

Do:
● Give some detail as to why you were good at them.

- Say if they tie in with what you would like to do within a career, for instance ICT and hence work with computers.

Don't:
- Appear blasé. 'I am just naturally gifted at most subjects.'
- Indicate you are not sure how on earth you achieved the results you did.
- Play down your achievements.

Example

I found I had a natural ability when learning languages. I found it relatively easy to understand the verbs and tenses and hence did really well. This isn't, however, something I want to continue with in my career, but am sure it will come in useful when travelling on holiday.

Which subjects did you least enjoy?

The subject you enjoyed least may well be the ones you found more difficult to study. There could be other reasons, such as you had a mixture of supply teachers and the learning was very disjointed, or you do not have a natural talent on the sports field, so physical education was difficult for you.

Do:
- Pick just one or two subjects that you can give some background detail to.
- State the learning/benefits from the studying subject.

Don't:
- Give a list of all the subjects you studied.
- State your teacher was horrible and didn't like you.

Example

I struggled with geography. We had a variety of teachers throughout my last couple of years, each with a different teaching style. I was only interested in minor elements of the subject, for instance the world and plants, but soil and oxbow lakes were not really my thing.

Don't arrive late and, even worse, without an apology. Poor candidates fail to put any obvious effort into their appearance, make poor eye contact, and arrive unprepared, without doing company research.

SANDRA FALCUS, HR MANAGER, PORTAKABIN

What made you choose the A levels you did?

People have different reasons for choosing the A levels they do, some go for the subjects they are better at to ensure good grades, others go for subjects that link in with their chosen degree and, potentially, their career.

Do:

- Give some rationale for your choice.
- Be honest. For example, if you weren't sure what career path to take, you chose subjects you enjoyed.

Example

My A level choice was driven by a variety of factors. I wanted to enjoy them for one, I had a good idea which career path to take and knew which A levels aligned to this, and the other reason was driven by the availability and timetabling of the subjects at my school. I know I chose well as I have received good grades and enjoyed the challenge – and it was a challenge.

Why did you do your A levels at college rather than continue with your education at school?

Some people do this by choice, others are forced to study outside of their school due to parents moving location, no sixth form facility being available, poor reputation for results or you just fancied a change of scenery. There are no right and wrong answers, but here a couple of things to consider:

- Explain clearly what the rationale was.
- If you did change because you wanted more autonomy and to be treated like a grown-up, then say so.

Example

I took the opportunity to move after my GCSEs as I wanted a change; I was also not particularly impressed with who would have been my teacher for geography so I decided to go to college. I really enjoyed the environment and having to take responsibility for your own learning and being out of the school arena.

Why are you applying for this role rather than going to university to study further?

The list could be endless and wide ranging, depending on your reasons, which may include the points given opposite.

- You may not want to continue studying as you have simply had enough of exams.
- You want to earn some money.
- You are considering going to university in a couple of years and you need to work in order to fund this.

Give some detail as to your rationale so as to persuade the interviewer you have given this some thought.

Example

I have really had enough of studying for the time being and am very keen to get some practical skills in the workplace and start my career. I also would like to earn some money, as I want to be able to buy my own home and car and be independent of my parents just as soon as I can manage it.

Why did you leave school after GCSEs, rather than carry on with your A levels?

It could be you hated school with a passion and couldn't face learning any more. You may well not be an academic and would have found A levels a challenge – A levels are not for everyone and they are not a prerequisite for every job. There could be a variety of reasons:

> **TOP TIP**
>
> Avoid giving single word answers to questions or shrugging off questions with 'I don't really know'. The interviewer only wants to get you chatting and find out all about you.

- You wanted to get out into the world of work and develop new skills.
- You didn't want to study any more, you aren't particularly academic and no specific subjects interested you enough to carry on.
- You moved away and the sixth form possibilities were limited in your new location – so you took the plunge to get into work.
- You decided to take an apprenticeship or Higher National Diploma (HND).

Example

I wanted to do get practical skills in the line of work I thought I was interested in. However, once I started on the building site I realised this just wasn't for me. I have since attended various computer courses and have really enjoyed learning about this area and this is where I want my career to be.

You left school without any qualifications, can you explain this?

You have progressed this far and got yourself an interview so you now need to convince the potential employer that you are the right person for the job and that your personality, qualities, skills and experiences far outweigh any academic qualifications – not an easy task!

Do:
- Think about your skills, qualities and experiences.
- Highlight any part-time jobs you have had.
- Communicate with enthusiasm and energy.
- Describe how your skills relate to the role you have applied for.
- Demonstrate a willingness to develop and learn on the job.

Don't:
- Dismiss qualifications as irrelevant.
- Play down the fact you haven't got any.
- Give reams of detail as to why you didn't achieve any results.
- Pass blame onto the educational system.

Example

I had some issues at school and really didn't enjoy the experience from start to finish. I found studying for exams really difficult and sadly decided to opt out of all of them – something now I deeply regret. I am currently rectifying this situation and revising hard to do my retake exams in the hope that I can achieve results that best reflect my academic ability.

4

Questions for graduates

As a qualified graduate it is important to be able to demonstrate the skills and experiences that you have gained at university as well as your academic achievement. Take time to think about the skills you have developed both at university as well as any employment undertaken or extracurricular activities you were involved in.

How do you feel you would settle into a work environment after four years' full-time study?

The interviewer wants to try to establish if you have given any thought to this and whether you recognise the difference between work and study. You may have worked throughout your degree so this will be easier for you to relate to. Whatever your situation, you need to be able to demonstrate how you would adapt to this new lifestyle. Consider indicating:

- That you are aware of the working hours and appreciate it is going to take time to adapt, but are looking forward to a more structured life.
- You worked throughout your degree studies so are looking forward to having to concentrate on just one thing.
- You are good at adapting to different circumstances.
- You don't underestimate the difference between study and full-time work.

Example

I don't underestimate the difference between the two and I am sure for the first couple of months I am going to be pretty tired from much longer working days and having to think and learn about what I am doing. I am really excited by this and keen to get started in my career.

Candidates shouldn't feel the need to give an answer if they don't have one – they may not have been in that situation before. Also, it takes a lot of guts to admit in an interview what areas for development a candidate has – however, hiring managers are often impressed when candidates recognise areas for improvement, and that they are doing something about it.

RESOURCING TEAM, VODAFONE UK

Getting your foot in the door

What has been the most useful experience from university that you can bring to the role?

They are not just looking for your academic achievements. You need to consider the wider aspects of what you did at university – these could range from being a member of a society to the discipline of studying and taking exams or being independent and living on your own. You need to describe:

● What the experience was.
● What you got out of the situation.
● How this is beneficial for the role/organisation.

Example

I have learnt a lot about myself while being away from home; taking responsibility for paying bills, setting up standing orders and doing my own cooking and cleaning have all benefited me in terms of taking responsibility. However, I think the most useful experience has been taking on the role as chair for the sailing club. I have learnt a lot about working with a team of people, setting goals and achieving results.

How do you feel your degree relates to the role?

You may have given careful consideration to your degree when you made your choice as it linked specifically into your choice of career, or it could be that you had no idea when you started your degree what you then wanted from a career – if the latter, you may need to do a good 'sell' on the connections between the two.

Example 1

I have always known I wanted to work with figures and data, hence the maths degree. I have a particular interest and strength in this area and enjoy the black/white aspects of dealing with numbers. I am now looking forward to using this in a career in accountancy.

Example 2

I realise there isn't an obvious link between my degree and my chosen career. At the time when I made my degree choice I really didn't know exactly what career path I wanted to take. However, I feel that the discipline of learning and achieving results demonstrates my determination and drive to achieve.

Which aspects of your degree did you find most challenging?

This could cover a variety of issues from the undisciplined approach of studying at university to the researching and production of your final year dissertation. Your reason may also be more specific in terms of subject areas within your degree, for example, if you studied English literature, perhaps there was a specific author you didn't enjoy. Be prepared for follow-on questions – these may include:

- Why was that?
- How did you overcome this?
- What did you learn from this?
- How have you applied this learning since?

Example

I guess the most challenging part was within my first year and getting used to working in teams with others – joint project work and making presentations as a team. This was something I had not experienced before and found the concept quite strange initially. However, I soon realised the benefits of this and how much more you can learn from other people.

> **TOP TIP**
>
> Turn any challenging aspects of your degree into a positive if you can; concentrate on what you got out of the challenging situations when studying, what you learnt.

How did you choose which university to attend?

The interviewer will be interested to assess your approach to decision making. How much research you did and what process you adopted to selecting a suitable institution. You may want to include:

- The research you undertook.
- What your priorities were, such as its extracurricular activities, location and reputation.

Avoid:

- Indicating, 'It was the first one I thought of', or 'My brother/sister went there.' These statements say very little about the thought process you adopted when choosing your university.

Example

I made a list of priorities. First of all it had to cover the degree I wanted to do, secondly I play sport so I wanted a university that had a good focus on sporting achievements and, third, I wanted to be within a two-hour train journey of home. Using these criteria I narrowed it down to three options and visited each one, getting a feel for the place and to see which suited me best. X was my preferred option and I was fortunate enough to obtain a place there.

Why did you choose to study the subject you did?

Some people have a clear idea of their chosen career and hence the degree course correlates with this. It may be you found the topic interesting or were particularly talented in this area, or you wanted to undertake a work placement year to get some practical work experience. Consider the following:

- Giving a clear rationale for your choice.
- Indicating the benefits of studying this subject.
- Indicating how pleased you are you chose the subject you did.
- Indicating anything you might have changed about your choice.

Example

I had always loved reading books as a child and found this interesting and enjoyable. By studying English literature I have managed to read a huge number of books across a range of authors and subject areas, enhancing my knowledge in all sorts of areas. I really enjoyed my degree and feel it will benefit me in my written communication skills in the workplace.

What was the most enjoyable part of your degree course?

The interviewer is interested to find out where your interests were and the type of areas you prefer to learn about or perhaps the way that you learn. It could be that you enjoyed the teamwork/project aspect of the course or the reading and research. This type of information can give the interviewer additional insight into your style. Consider the following:

- The part of the course you enjoyed best and why you like doing it – give some depth of rationale.
- Highlighting the benefits of this.
- How you intend to use this learning.

Avoid:
- Making flippant comments such as 'I enjoyed the partying' and 'only having a few hours lectures a week' – you may be making a joke, but it may not come over as such.

Example

I really enjoyed researching and putting together my dissertation. I chose a subject that really inspired me, which made the learning so much more interesting and enjoyable. I planned and prepared the work well and found it useful to give myself some timescales and milestones. When I handed it in I had a great sense of satisfaction and achievement, I felt I couldn't have done any more.

Was there anything about your course that you found difficult/ struggled with?

The interviewer may not necessarily be interested in the specific subject area but studying as a whole. The answer has to be 'yes' or 'no', but you will need to back this up with further information.

Example 1
There was nothing really that I struggled with particularly. Some subject areas were more interesting than others and some of the teams we worked with were more challenging at times due to differing personalities, but nothing that became a real issue.

Example 2
There was one element that I found difficult to grasp at first, I guess these things happen. I realised that if I didn't take some action I was going to get into difficulty so I arranged a meeting with my tutor – this resolved the issue and although it was still not my strongest area I understood the basic principles and was able to apply them.

With the benefit of hindsight, would you choose to study the same course again? If not, why not?

The interviewer is interested to find out your ability to self-reflect and learn from experiences. You may want to consider:

● If your answer is 'yes', then highlight the benefits of the course you did.
● If your answer is 'no', then explain your rationale for this.

Example
I really enjoyed my course and was fortunate enough to meet and study with some great people. However, I do think that if I were to have done this again I would either have chosen an additional subject to work alongside my degree, such as a language or creative writing, or I would have chosen a subject that involved an industrial placement. I think the benefits and the hands-on experience you would get from this are exceptional.

What vacation work did you take on while at university and how did you obtain this?

Not only is the interviewer interested to know the type of vacation work you undertook and how you secured this, but also what the benefits of this were and what you learnt. It is sometimes not just the money that drives you to get work but the need and desire to gain experience, for instance in customer service skills, planning and organising and taking responsibility.

Getting your foot in the door

It may well be you wanted to gain experience within your chosen career path or you needed something that would make ends meet. Consider answering the following:

- What attracted you to the work you did?
- How did you obtain this?
- What have you learnt from this experience?
- What aspects did you enjoy most?
- What didn't you like?

How did you fund your degree/course?

The interviewer is trying to establish how driven you are to achieve results. You may have been fortunate enough to have been funded 100 per cent by parents throughout your degree or you had to work as many hours as you could. Interviewers are often interested in people who can demonstrate their desire to work and achieve results rather than those that have been handed everything on a plate.

Do:
- Describe how you planned the funding of your degree, such as understanding how much money you needed and working hours available during your studies.
- Explain what actions you took to ensure you could undertake your studies; for example, work during your studies, vacation work.
- Include what you feel you have gained from this experience.

Don't:
- State you didn't have to work as your parents paid for everything.
- State you would rather have a bigger overdraft than having to work.

How did you manage your time when studying and working part-time?

This is a good opportunity to explain to the interviewer your ability to plan, prioritise and organise your time. You need to consider the following:

- The actions you took to plan how you fitted in work and study. You could include using a diary, timetabling of events and projects.
- What the benefits were of doing this.
- What the learning has been from this.

Example

I recognised financially I needed to work and also wanted to have interaction with different people other than those I lived and studied with. When I went for the interview I was very clear as to the hours I could work and took my study timetable with me. I was fortunate enough that they accepted this. I used a diary to keep track of my project deadlines, listing when my lectures were and also what shifts I was allocated at work. I have been successful in being able to handle both work and study.

How would you describe your contribution when working on team projects at university?

The interviewer wants to understand how you have worked in teams and what your role has been within these. You may want to consider the following:

- What role(s) you have undertaken.
- What contributions/differences you have made to the team(s).
- How you overcame any challenges with other team members.
- What you have learnt from these experiences.
- What you have enjoyed/not enjoyed from these experiences.

Example

I guess I am the type of person who likes to get everybody together and organises meeting up and keeping on track of progress to meet the deadlines. I also make a good contribution to the creative elements of projects and enjoy the putting together of presentations, for instance making the visuals look good. There was an occasion when one person kept not turning up for meetings and I asked if he had any problems as it was causing an issue with others who had to do their work. It turned out he was struggling with the topic so a couple of us gave him more support. We ended up with a really good result.

What made you think that university was right for you?

The interviewer is interested in the thought process you adopted when making the decision about further education or work. This can say a lot about the type of person you are. You may want to consider the dos and don'ts as well as the example overleaf.

Do:

- Be honest. If you didn't know what else you wanted to do, say so.
- State you were completely clear you want to be X and needed to obtain the degree in order to do this.
- Look at the wider benefits of university, such as living independently, managing budgets, meeting new people.

Don't:

- Say that you wanted to read books for three years.

Example

I have to be honest and say I was really undecided as to what career path I wanted to take. I felt that going to university would give me more options and wider experiences in terms of living away from home, managing my own budget, meeting new people and raising my studying to another level. I have really enjoyed my time at university but am now ready to put it all into practice and get into the real world.

How are you managing to complete your final exams and dissertation while job searching and attending interviews?

The interviewer is trying to establish how you are managing your time. Exams and interviews can be stressful situations and how you deal with this and prepare for both can be very interesting to a future employer.

Do:

- Explain how you have planned your time.
- Detail the preparation you have undertaken for interviews, such as answers to questions.
- Explain how you are managing the stress/pressure. For instance, through good planning and preparation, so avoiding last-minute rush and panic.
- Explain how you have dealt with any issues you have faced.

Don't:

- Be flippant or playing down the situation – lots of people have been in this situation and it is tough.
- Give them the impression that you don't care or are flying by the seat of your pants.

Example

I really didn't appreciate how difficult it was going to be. I have planned my dissertation well but I have had to face a few hiccups, for one my laptop decided to misbehave and I lost about 7,000 words. I have just had to work really long hours to get myself back on track. I have prepared a few answers to questions for my interviews as I feel this is really helpful and helps to alleviate any last-minute anxieties. I created my revision timetable as soon as exam dates were released so these were written in my diary and from this I know exactly where I am – I'm just hoping it all pays off.

What was the reason for your choice of studying part-time rather than taking a full-time course?

The interviewer is trying to establish your rationale for this. A very simple and straightforward response is needed, so avoid going into in-depth detail. It could be that you have a good job with part-time hours that you didn't want to lose. You need to:

- State clearly your rationale.
- Stick to the facts.
- Avoid going into lots of detail.

Example

I didn't really have a lot of choice. I have been my mother's carer for the last four years and needed be around every morning and evening to look after her.

How difficult did you find returning to education as a mature student? How did you cope with this?

The interviewer wants to find out how you handled any difficulties, the approach you took and what you learnt from this situation. This will be a good indicator as to how well you will adapt to joining a new position with the company. Some issues or benefits may have been:

- Most people were much younger – different thought processes and interests.
- It was a long time since you had undertaken an academic discipline and it was difficult getting back into reading documents and writing essays.
- You couldn't quite keep up with the partying scene!
- You were able to remain detached from some of the 'relationship' issues that occurred in groups.

You may want to include:

- How you overcame any issues.
- The overall benefits of attending university – what you got out of the experience.
- What you were able to contribute as a mature student.

Getting your foot in the door

What learning did you gain at university/college other than your academic studies that you think will be useful at work?

The interviewer wants to understand the bigger picture. What extracurricular activities you undertook and what experiences you gained from them. These could range from being a member of a sports team to chair of the student union. Look at the wider skills and experiences you gained from these. You could include leading others, team working, communicating, influencing and planning and organising. It could be something as simple as learning to be independent, cooking, cleaning and paying the bills. Ensure you include:

- The activities you were involved in.
- What contributions you made.
- How these will be beneficial to the workplace – transferable skills.
- What you learnt from these experiences.
- How you will apply this learning in the workplace.

Example

I was vice chair of the sociology society and I captained the university chess team. Both positions have enabled me to gain valuable skills including organisation, leading and supporting others and learning how to plan and organise events. There was also a strong element of having to take responsibility for making things happen, something that I am keen to do at work.

What are the three most important things you have learnt from your internship/work experience?

This question is your chance to express your personality and perhaps a sense of humour, but ensure you keep it at an appropriate level. It is important that you are able to expand as they are not looking for a three-word answer. Explain the learning and why it was important. You need to:

- Keep to three things only.
- Explain each learning point and why it was important to you.
- Be prepared to give some detail.

Example

One, I learnt that it is really important to listen to others as they have different and sometimes better ideas. Two, ask lots of questions in order to check and clarify information and three, you learn something new every day. I guess really in summary that is, ask, listen and learn.

Lots of people have degrees these days, what makes you different from the rest?

This is your chance for a sales pitch. You need to highlight your attributes, skills and experiences and convince them of your fit within their organisation.

Do:
- Highlight your skills and experiences.
- Use a range of positive adjectives that describe you well.
- Align your skills to those of the role and the culture of the organisation.
- Sound confident, enthusiastic and interested.

Don't:
- Make a statement and not follow this through with specific facts.
- Appear disinterested or not bothered by the outcome.
- Reel off a list of skills that have nothing to do with the role or the organisational culture.

Example

Not only do I have a high level degree, I have developed a range of skills throughout my studies. Through my continuous part-time positions I can demonstrate my strong work ethic coupled with my ability to plan and organise my time efficiently. I work well with others and have been able to do this through the various clubs and societies I have been involved in. I am keen to learn and develop further, something that your company advocates.

You only got a third-class degree, why should we choose you when we are looking for someone with a second-class or above?

As with the previous question, you need to do a very good sales pitch concentrating on your skills and qualities rather than your academic qualifications. There may also be a very good reason why you got a third-class degree and you will need to explain this. However, avoid getting into detail and making excuses for the result. Some of the reasons could have been:

- Family bereavement.
- Illness.
- Undergoing re-marking at present.
- Only missed a second class by one point.

Don't:
- Make pathetic excuses.
- Blame others.

> **REMEMBER!**
>
> *Don't make excuses or blame others if you didn't get the degree grade you would have liked. Highlight your personal qualities and skills and describe what an asset you will be to their organisation.*

Getting your foot in the door

Why did you leave your degree part way through the course?

There could be a variety of reasons for this and you need to be able to give a clear rationale. Some of these reasons could be:

- Family situation, such as a bereavement, care for family member.
- Funding issues.
- Didn't enjoy the course.
- University just wasn't for you.
- Was offered a full-time job and at the time it was too good an opportunity not to take.

Example

To a point the situation was out of my hands. For one, I wasn't really enjoying the degree topic I had chosen. Second, my sister was very ill and I lived three hours away from home. This was proving difficult not only for me but my parents too, as they needed my support. And third, for that same reason I needed to earn some money as my studying was a drain on their resources. However, the benefits of doing this were that I gained some valuable work experience and spent time with my family.

Are you considering taking a gap year at any point?

The interviewer wants to establish how long you are likely to be around. Recruiting someone can be time consuming and expensive and the company wants to know that their money isn't going to be wasted. You need to convince the interviewer that you are planning on being there for some time. If this is a temporary position, then your answer may be different – it may be you are working to save for a gap year.

If the answer is 'yes', then:
- Be careful with the truth – they are not going to employ you if you are planning to leave in the short term (if applying for a permanent role).
- Indicate you are saving up to go travelling and indicate how long it is likely to be before you go, for example, 18 months' time.

If the answer is 'no', then:
- State your reason for this.
- Avoid getting into in-depth conversations.
- Avoid making any jealous comments such as, 'It's alright for some, some of us have got to get a job.'

Why didn't you take a gap year?

There could be a variety of reasons for this. Keep it brief and state the facts. Avoid getting into long conversations or appearing bitter towards those that have been fortunate enough to go travelling. It may be that you are really not interested and want to wait until you can afford to do it in style. Some of your responses could include:

- 'Didn't have enough money to go.'
- 'Want to get into work and gain some skills and experience.'
- 'Not interested at the moment.'
- 'Would rather wait until I am older and I can travel in comfort.'
- 'I want to really get my teeth stuck into work and use my degree effectively.'

Example

The situation and opportunity has never arisen. I am involved at a high level in playing tennis for my university and now my county. I don't want to miss out on any competitions over the next few years and I really enjoy this. I can travel any time in the future, but I won't be able to play tennis at the level I do forever.

What did you achieve in your gap year?

The interviewer is looking to gain an insight into what you achieved in terms of skills and experiences and how you can use these in the workplace. Look beyond the bungee jump and the physical travelling and think about your specific achievements. These could range from:

- Being responsible – arranging own travel from A to B.
- Using your initiative and reacting to situations and problems.
- Meeting and working with a variety of different people from varied cultures.
- Being independent of friends and family.
- Planning and organising.

Example

I gained a lot in terms of becoming far more independent than I was before, taking responsibility for my safety and arranging my travel through ten different countries. I have gained in confidence in terms of communicating with different people from all walks of life and a willingness to turn my hand to anything. I also had to plan ahead in terms of accommodation and arranging route plans. I had a great time but am now ready to get my head down and focus on my career.

Getting your foot in the door

For school leavers and graduates

The following questions apply to both school leavers and graduates and explore experiences you may have gained outside of your studies, your career aims and reasons for applying for a particular training scheme or job.

....

How can this job help you achieve your career goals?

This is being asked to establish your understanding of the role you have applied for, how this relates to your own studies and qualities and how this fits in with your career aims. You may be using this as a stepping stone to get to where you want to be and need the experience, but it is important to emphasise how keen you are to work for the company and this is not just any old job. You need to:

- Link this job to your ultimate career goals.
- Identify you are keen to gain experience in the workplace.
- Build on your skills and experiences to date.
- Indicate you want to work for an organisation like this one as they are keen to develop and train their staff.
- Demonstrate a clear understanding of your career path and how the company fits into this.

Example

I am really keen to progress within my career and consider every role and job I do as a contributory factor towards this. It is very important to gain different experiences and skills as I move from role to role or to different organisations.

What work did you undertake during term time and why did you choose the kind of work you did while undertaking your studies?

They are trying to establish if you had a clear rationale for choosing the work you did or if you took any work you could get. Some people like to be working in an environment that they can relate specifically to their degree, others focus more around what fits in with their studies and some maybe because they can get some good discounts such as in bars, clubs and shops.

> **TOP TIP**
>
> Whatever work experience you undertook during your studies it is important to highlight the skills you obtained while you were there.

Example

The jobs available to me at the time of doing my degree that were within walking distance and fitted in with my lectures were really limited, so I was lucky to obtain the job I did. When I started I worked as a shop assistant at X. This was great because I developed face to face customer service skills as well as receiving a really good staff discount. I was soon promoted to supervisor, which has given me the opportunity to develop some coaching and mentoring skills – something I really quite enjoyed.

How did you prepare for your exams and if you were to study for your exams again, what would you do differently?

This is a good opportunity to demonstrate your planning, prioritising and organisational skills. You may have learnt from mistakes over the past few years and it is important to highlight these learning points within your response.

Do:
- Describe the approach you took in preparation.
- Indicate what methodologies you used, such as a timetable, diary, spreadsheet.
- Detail the revision techniques you used; for instance, mind mapping, reading, note taking.
- Say how you prioritised your time and allocated extra time for contingencies.
- Identify any learning from previous revision and study periods.

Don't:
- Give lots of detail around what subjects you tackled first.
- Be flippant. 'I was fortunate to know my subject well and hence needed little revision' sounds like you are rather full of yourself.
- State you did nothing on the planning and just went with the flow.

Example
I learnt a big lesson from my AS/first year exams and applied this learning for subsequent exams. I hadn't left enough time and had not appreciated how much I needed to go back and read again in order to refresh my learning. I went on to take a much more structured approach, creating a timetable for my revision and sticking to this as much as possible. I also did more revision throughout each term and I was disciplined in terms of cutting down on social activities, but appreciated I still needed time to switch off.

I see you played sport at school/college, how did you contribute to the team?

The interviewer is interested to know what you contributed in terms of the team rather than the specific position you played within the team. Focus on the broader skills that you developed. Consider the ideas overleaf.

Getting your foot in the door

- Identify your contribution as a team member. This could include that you always attended training sessions, offered support and coaching to new members of the team, and were motivational and encouraging in times when the team were not winning.
- Took responsibility for collecting subscriptions – acted as treasurer during your last year.
- Actively involved in the fundraising activities.
- Acted as vice captain when needed.

Example

I feel I made an active contribution to the team as a whole. Not only did I regularly turn up at training and take responsibility for collecting monies and ensuring everyone knew when matches were taking place, but I also offered some technical coaching and tactics to new members and acted as vice captain when needed. I was also a really good centre half.

I see you were involved in the Duke of Edinburgh Award scheme. What did you learn from this and what did you enjoy most about it?

The Duke of Edinburgh Award scheme is highly regarded within businesses. It demonstrates that you have contributed in some way towards team goals and achieved some personal successes in addition to your studies.

Do:
- Identify your learning from the experiences you undertook.
- Identify how this learning has benefited you or will benefit you in the workplace.
- Identify what you enjoyed and give some rationale as to why.
- Highlight some of the key experiences and tasks you undertook.

Don't:
- Highlight a situation if you failed to achieve the task, unless you can identify some good learning opportunities from this.
- Just list all of the activities you undertook with little other evidence of how you benefited from these and what you learnt.

Example

I particularly enjoyed the four-day expedition we undertook across Dartmoor. It was really challenging in terms of physical and mental ability and also ensuring we achieved our goal. We encountered problems when one of our team members hurt her ankle. We were able to distribute her luggage between us and I established another route we could take, which ensured we met

our goal by missing out some of the rougher terrain that would have caused her problems.
I learnt that there is always a way around a problem, you just need to stay focused on the
task in hand.

What were the biggest challenges you faced when taking part in the Young Enterprise Scheme?

The interviewer wants to establish how you have dealt with any challenges and your specific role and contribution in this. Due to the variety of tasks that you can undertake within the scheme you have a fairly good choice of examples to pull on. Choose something that you personally found challenging, rather than the team, or if you are only able to use a team example, make sure you focus on your specific contribution and input within this.

Example
When we were undertaking our entrepreneurial task we had some issues within the team. Some members wanted one product and others another product. I had been voted as sales director of the team. I managed to analyse all of the data we had put together on both products and broke this information down in terms of production time, sales revenue and ultimately profit margins. I was able to persuade some of the members of the group through using this information rather than becoming emotionally involved in what was the best idea. It was challenging as there were some pretty strong characters within the team but by using factual information this alleviated any further issues or arguments.

Were you happy with the results you achieved at university/school and what could you have done to achieve better results?

This is obviously a personal response; you either were or were not. If you achieved all As/A★s and a first class degree then perhaps the answer will be, 'Yes you are very happy.' If you feel there was room for improvement, then state where and how this could have been achieved. Consider:

- Backing up your initial response with some reasoning.
- Avoiding listing all your results and going through each one.
- Picking out the more obvious ones.
- Not passing blame for some poorer results – take it on the chin.
- Striking a balance in terms of good and poor results.
- Giving some tangible actions as to what you could have done better.

Example 1
Generally I was really pleased with the results I obtained with both my GCSEs and A levels.

I feel this is a good representation of my ability and how hard I studied. I did my best and don't feel I could have done any more.

Example 2

I was really quite disappointed with my results as I don't feel this gives a good indication as to my real ability. I know I could have done better and this has been a good learning experience I guess. What I should have done is created a much more rigorous revision timetable and stuck to it. I am currently retaking two of my exams in order to better my results.

> **REMEMBER!**
>
> *When you are asked about your results, the interviewer is trying to establish your ability to reflect on your abilities and identify any learning opportunities.*

We have had problems in the past taking on school leavers/new graduates. Why do you think it would be different with you?

The interviewer may have experienced problems with individuals who find it difficult to integrate into work life, are arrogant about their own abilities or are just not that interested in working, they just want the money. In your answer:

- Indicate that you are aware from friends/other employers that there can be difficulties with some school leavers or new graduates integrating into the workplace.
- Indicate how you would work to overcome any of these difficulties.
- Indicate why you are different to other graduates/school leavers.

Example

I know that some graduates get a bad reputation for being arrogant about their abilities in the workplace when really they know very little. I think the fact that I have already had plenty of work experience would help me in this respect as it has made me less naïve about what is expected at work. I also would like to think that I have good interpersonal skills and would recognise if someone at work had a problem with me.

Why do you want to be part of our graduate/management trainee programme/apprentice scheme and what benefits do you think there are to participating in a programme like this?

Schemes such as this usually give you the opportunity to work across many areas of an organisation, develop skills and gain a proper understanding of the industry you are working in. They can be an excellent introduction to working life and a great way of getting a foot in the door of a reputable employer. So in your answer think of including the ideas opposite.

- Indicate why you would like to be part of the scheme.
- Demonstrate an understanding of the particular scheme this employer offers.
- Describe the key benefits there would be for you.

Example

I see this scheme as an excellent introduction to the company and a great opportunity to work in a variety of different departments. This approach is helpful in making a final career choice, but also ensures that whatever part of the organisation you do end up in that you have a good appreciation of others' point of view or work demands. It is also a good opportunity to learn from others and develop a whole new range of skills.

What qualities do you think we are looking for in our graduate/ management trainees/apprentices?

This varies from one organisation to another so it is important that you have a clear idea about this particular one before attending for interview. There will be information available on the company's website, scheme promotional material and even in the interview invitation.

The one common factor will be that the company is looking to take on people who have the potential and desire to learn and develop in the long term. Employers see schemes like this as a good way of bringing new, inexperienced people into the organisation.

Example

I think you are looking to take people onto this scheme who are keen to learn and develop, who can demonstrate an aptitude for working in this industry and are prepared to be flexible and move around the organisation a bit. I guess also people who are willing to get stuck in and do the work.

What additional activities were you involved in outside of school/ university?

Employers are always interested to learn about what you have done in addition to your studies. This may include sports or social clubs, raising money for charity, paid or voluntary work or hobbies. They will feel that this says something about the kind of person you are. In your answer indicate:

- What the additional activities were.
- Why it was important for you to do these.
- Whether or not you are going to continue with these activities once in full-time employment.

Getting your foot in the door

Example

While at university I have been involved with a charity project raising money to take disadvantaged children away on activity holidays. I felt that it was important to put something back into the local community having had a fairly privileged upbringing. I have found this work very rewarding and will maintain some involvement in it once I am working.

How have you benefited from your involvement from extracurricular activities?

It is also important to be able to identify what you learnt, what skills you developed or how you benefited personally from your extracurricular activities. Consider including the following in your answer:

● Describing what you learnt.
● Indicating the skills you developed.
● How the skills you developed will be useful in the job you have applied for.
● Any other benefits.

Example

Raising money for a charity and working closely with others has taught me the importance of teamwork and being organised. We were all volunteers so it was vital to make the most of the time we had available to us. I also learnt a lot about how other people live and the difficulties they face. An additional benefit has been to make some great new friends, people I know I will stay in touch with for many years to come.

If you could do any job, what would it be?

Probably used to lighten the mood of the interview, this question allows you to say just about anything. Whatever your dream job is, indicate why you would like it and why you haven't gone for it.

Example

My dream job would to be a ranger in a game park in Africa somewhere. I am fascinated by the continent and the animals that live there and would love to work closely with them, protecting them for the future of the planet. I guess the only reason I haven't done this is it would require living in the middle of nowhere, but I will definitely spend a holiday one day learning all about this.

What interests you in this job?

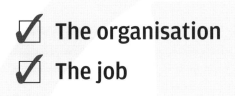

☑ **The organisation**

☑ **The job**

The organisation

Demonstrating you have a particular interest in the organisation and the job, and that it's not just another application, can be an important way of setting yourself apart from other candidates. Interviewers will want to assess how much research you have done before turning up for the interview, whether you have understood what they are about as an organisation and, most importantly, if you know what the role will require you to do (see pages 82–8).

Why would you like a role in our organisation?

The interviewers want to know that their company has a special attraction to you – it's not just another job application. To answer this question you will need to know something about the organisation and be able to describe why you think it is an interesting place to work. Your reasons might include:

- The organisation is successful and you would like to play a part in it.
- You know they are a small/large organisation and feel this would suit you.
- They place a lot of emphasis upon training their staff and you would like to be involved in this.
- They are a well-known brand and you would like to experience working for such a company.
- They have a strong team/quality/customer service culture and this is the kind of environment you like to work in.

> ## REMEMBER!
>
> *Just think about when you meet someone for the first time – you are a lot more interested in a person who shows an interest in you.*

Avoid:
- Indicating that you don't know very much about them.
- Commenting on the job – they are not asking about this.

> An ideal candidate is someone who looks to establish empathy with the interviewer; someone who has genuinely planned and researched the organisation and the role that they are interviewing for. During the course of the interview, the candidate will ideally make an effort to provide specific evidence, with detailed examples, that demonstrate how they believe their previous or current experience and aptitude maps closely on to the opportunity.
>
> SOPHIE MILLIKEN, MANAGER, RECRUITMENT, JOHN LEWIS

What have you found out about our organisation?

It is important to demonstrate that you have put some effort into finding out about the company before applying for the job or attending for interview. In your answer describe:

- What research you have done.
- What you have found out about the organisation.
- What you liked about what you found out about the organisation.

Don't:

- Say you have done research by looking on the website, for example, if you haven't – they are bound to ask you further questions and will know you are making it up.
- Restrict your answer to reciting facts about the organisation – make sure you comment on what impression it has made upon you.

Example

Before coming along for this interview I did some research by looking on your website and also went and visited some of your premises to get a better understanding of the service you provide. It would appear that you have grown significantly as an organisation over the last few years and been very successful. What I found really interesting was the emphasis you put upon the quality of work rather that just making money – it is refreshing to find that these days.

> ### TOP TIP
>
> **Employers' pet hates include:**
>
> - A candidate who has made no effort to find out anything about the organisation or the job.
> - Someone saying, 'I had a quick look on the website' – they are paying lip service to research.
> - Candidates who confuse the company with one that has a similar name.
> - Candidates who can't remember which job it is they are being interviewed for – they have applied for so many.

What do you think of our website?

You said you had looked at it so now you have to prove it. Comment upon how useful you found it as a candidate and also a potential customer of the organisation.

Do:

- Make positive comments about the information you found there.
- Indicate whether or not you found it easy to use.
- Make brief, specific comments about anything particularly interesting you found on the site.

What interests you in this job?

Don't:
- Be damning of the whole thing or give a list of all of the things that you didn't like about it.

Example

I had a look at the job vacancy section of the site and found the section with videos by existing employees talking about their work really interesting. I think overall the site looks good and was easy to navigate. I am sure your customers find it a useful source of information.

How do you think our website could be improved?

The interviewer is not expecting you to be a web design expert – unless, of course, that is the job you have gone for. They are interested in any thoughts you have on the site as a user and also, of course, using another kind of question to check out whether or not you really did look at the website.

If you have any thoughts, then share them – they may be about layout, content or how easy it was to use. If you haven't got any ideas on how it could be changed, then say so and make some positive comments about what you thought about it.

Example

On the whole I found the website very useful; there was a lot of information about your products and services. The job vacancy section was quite interesting, but it would have been helpful to look at job descriptions or summaries of the roles you have vacant at the moment in order to gain a better understanding.

You say you have read our company literature, what do you think about it?

Again this is your opportunity to demonstrate that you have done some research into the company. Comment on what literature you looked at, where you got it from and how useful you found it. Comment on the information from the point of view of a candidate and a potential customer as this will show you have given it some thought.

Example

The brochures I was sent were really helpful in giving me an understanding of your business and how you work with your customers. I hadn't realised that you had offices in so many European countries and I like your passion as an organisation around providing good customer service.

Have you any suggestions as to how we could improve our company image?

Even if you are not an expert on this area, use your own experience and comment on the company's image from a candidate's point of view. Answers might include:

- You are not terribly well known to most of the general public so for applicants it would be helpful to have more information in the advertisement about who you are and what you do.
- As a recent graduate you were not a name that I was familiar with – you may find it beneficial to raise your profile at universities and colleges as an employer.
- You have large premises locally but don't seem to be terribly active in the local community. I know a lot of companies have found this a good way of raising their profile as an employer and as a business.

Don't:
- Give a flat 'no'.
- Indicate that their marketing and image is terrible.
- Indicate they have a bad reputation as an employer.

Are you familiar with any of our products and services?

Try to say more than a simple 'yes' or 'no'! Your answers might include:

- They are not something I have used myself, but since seeing this job advertised I have done some research into them.
- Yes, I am a big fan and have been a customer for years, that's why I would really like this job.
- I know a lot of people who think very highly of the services you provide.

Don't:
- Indicate that you know nothing about their products or services.
- Make something up – they will be able to tell you are doing this.

What comments do you have on our products/services?

If you have any thoughts on what is good, or could be improved, then now is the time to say so. It will demonstrate that you have thought about what their business is about and what they offer to their customers.

Example

Your products seem to be in quite a niche market, which is good – there is limited competition from other companies and I would guess this means you have the opportunity to make a reasonable profit margin on each item. I wonder in the future whether you will also develop more mainstream products and, therefore, open up a wider marketplace for yourselves.

How would you rate us against our competitors?

By asking you this question, the interviewer is assessing your knowledge of the marketplace and their company's place with in it. In your answer, try to give your views on how you believe they are placed against competitors rather than just repeating what you have read or heard about them.

Example

It is clear that many of your services are of a higher quality than those of your competitors – not only are you known for this, but it is easy to see this as a user. At the moment you are not charging a premium price for this level of quality and I wonder, as your name becomes better known, whether this is something you will be able to do in the future to ensure the continued success of the company.

What advantages do you think we have above others in the marketplace?

Focus your answer on two or three aspects that you perceive to be an advantage. These might include:

- A good reputation as an organisation and as an employer.
- Are very well known and have a long track record.
- A family run company that people like to support.
- A good range of products or services.
- Innovative approach to offering services.
- The backing of a much larger organisation that owns the business.

What is the worst thing you have heard about our company?

This question could be another way of testing your knowledge of the company and what research you have completed. Keep this brief and top level, avoid getting into too much detail around the whys and wherefores and also avoid giving an opinion or identifying individuals within an organisation – keep it factual. Comments could be about the suggestions given opposite.

- Making people redundant.
- A drop in sales in quarter x.
- Staff complaints about uniform requirements.
- People disagreeing with the new branding that was recently launched.
- Delivery issues.

Example

I have to be honest and say that I have not heard anything untoward about your company in recent months. A friend of mine has worked here for some years and is a great advocate of the culture and products you produce. I was aware that you were in the position last year of having to make some redundancies but lots of companies have to restructure and re-evaluate their spending at some time or another.

TOP TIP

When talking about anything bad you've heard about the interviewer's company:

- Avoid giving a list of issues and poor press.
- Keep it brief and to the point.
- Turn negative comments into positive ones whenever you can.

What interests you in this job?

The job

This section covers the questions that you may be asked about the job you have applied for and provides some guidance on the kind of information you should be familiar with to provide strong, convincing answers. Finding out more about the organisation and the role will also enable you to make a further assessment of whether or not it is the job for you – let's face it, you may find something out at this stage that would put you off continuing with the selection process.

....

What interests you in this particular role?

The interviewer wants to know that you have a genuine interest in doing this job. Think about why you like the sound of it and why you think you might be good at it. In your answer consider including:

- Three or four points about the job that interest you.
- Indicate why it is a good match for your existing skills.
- Any longer term aims it will help you fulfil.
- How it will fit well with your approach to work/life balance.

Example

I am particularly interested in this role as I think it is a good match for my skills and sounds like an exciting challenge. From what you have said it would also provide me with some opportunity to develop further and maybe progress within the company in the future. I live locally so it would be easy for me to get here on time and I would enjoy working for a local employer and being part of the local business community.

What are the key responsibilities of the role?

The interviewer wants to be sure that you have a good understanding of what the job entails and there are no misunderstandings about what you will be required to do. There will be clues in the job advertisement and anything they have told you about the position. They may have even sent you some information about the role when they invited you for interview. In your answer:

- List the key responsibilities of the job as you understand them.
- Ask them to indicate if they feel you have missed anything important.

> **TOP TIP**
>
> If you feel unsure about what the job entails before going for the interview, then ring up and ask. There is nothing worse than making all that effort to go to the interview and then finding out it's not the job you thought it was.

What skills and qualities are critical to this role?

This question gives you a great opportunity to not only comment on the skills and qualities required for the role, but also indicate how good a match they are with your skills and qualities. You can probably make an educated guess about what they will be looking for, but don't forget to also refer back to any information you have about the job. In your answer:

- Give a brief summary of the skills and knowledge that are needed.
- Give a brief summary of the kind of personal qualities you think will be useful in the role.
- Describe how these link to your own skills and qualities.

Example

From what I have found out about the job I would say that the ability to work well with customers and colleagues and provide excellent service, good attention to detail and very good technology skills are the key things required. In addition, I think you would need to be an outgoing person who enjoys interacting with people a lot. I feel that I have developed many of these skills in my last job and am particularly praised for my strong IT skills and ability to build relationships with customers.

What are you looking for in an employer?

Describe the things that are important to you in an employer when you are deciding whether or not to take a job. These may vary from the development opportunities they offer and the scope for future progression through to their reputation as an employer and how well they pay. In your answer:

Do:
- Indicate two or three things that are important to you.
- Describe why these things are important to you.
- Pick things that you know this company will be able to offer you.
- Make a clear link between what you are looking for and what you think this company can offer.

Example

In looking for a new employer it is really important to me to find one that provides good opportunities for future development, that likes to keep staff for the long term and values team working. I really enjoy working with colleagues and like to build long-term relationships with them. I can see from your company literature that these things are all very important to you as an organisation.

What are you looking for in a new role?

Don't just say, 'A new challenge.' Explain the kind of thing you would see as a challenge or any other factors that are important to you in a new job. Your answers may include, the opportunity to:

- Learn something new.
- Use the skills you have developed.
- Work in a different industry.
- Work as part of a large/small team.
- Work independently.
- Run a budget.
- Manage a team.
- Be creative.
- Interact more with customers.

> **REMEMBER!**
>
> *Describe things that you know the job will provide. There's no point saying you want to have the opportunity to work independently if you know this is a team-based role.*

Example

I really want to use my creative skills more as I have developed some good ideas in my last role that have been implemented and received well. I would like to develop these even further in a different company and environment.

What other organisations have you applied to?

It is probably not necessary, or even wise, to name names, but just give a broad indication of the types of organisations you have applied to. The interviewer is seeking information on what kinds of companies you are interested in working for, assessing how focused you are being in your job search and whether or not you are serious about this application.

Example

I have applied to a couple of other organisations – all of them in a similar sector to yourselves and looking to grow their staff numbers significantly over the next few years. I have to say that your company sounds like the most structured and organised and more like my kind of place to work.

> **TOP TIP**
>
> A good way to close your answer is to say something about how positive you feel about working for this company.

How does this job compare to others that you have applied for?

In your answer tread a fine line between being honest and diplomatic. There is nothing wrong in saying you have been for other interviews and whether or not you are seriously interested in them. However, if you do want a job offer from this company, indicate that your preference would be for this role.

Example 1
The other jobs that I have gone for don't provide the opportunity to work in such a large team or face to face with customers. I think I would learn a lot more in this job and have better opportunities to develop in the longer term.

Example 2
This role would provide me with far more autonomy and responsibility, being able to work and contribute at a more strategic level than the others I have applied to.

Have you received any job offers from any other company?
Again it's a balance between being totally honest and diplomatic. If you say 'yes', be prepared to say a little more – they may go on to ask if the salary is similar, if you have accepted the job, or question how interested you are in their vacancy. State clearly your interest in this role if that is genuinely the case.

Example
I did receive an offer from another firm the other day, but was keen to come along today and learn more about this opportunity as I felt it was probably more suitable for me. I have really enjoyed learning more about the position and am keen to progress my application further if you feel I am the right person for the job.

How do you ensure that you stay up to date with what is going on in the industry?
Describe the key sources of information you use to ensure that you keep up to date with what is going on. These may include:

- The internet.
- Trade magazines or websites.
- Networking with colleagues in other companies.
- Newspapers and television.

Also, indicate how often you do this and whether or not you take a structured approach to keeping in touch – maybe doing something once a week.

Example
I subscribe to two trade journals and also belong to a business group where I have the opportunity of discussing current issues with colleagues from other organisations. I find by doing this I am able to keep up to date and formulate my own ideas about things we should be doing at work to improve business opportunities in order to keep up with our competitors.

What do you think are the major challenges within this industry?

Here is a more testing question about your understanding of the industry you work in and an important one to give a confident answer to. In your answer:

● Focus upon one or two challenges.
● Give some indication as to how you, or your organisation, is tackling these challenges.

Avoid:
● Stating something you can't then substantiate or don't have any ideas about how it could be tackled – they are bound to ask you.

Example
I think the key challenges in the retail industry are to maximise profits at a time when sales are down and margins are at their lowest for years. To help this I do everything I can to make sure that my stores are keeping an eye on staff costs as well as the less obvious things like heating and lighting costs and focusing on cross selling to the customers that are shopping with them.

What do you think will be the future opportunities for the industry over the next few years?

The answer you give will be dependent upon the level you are operating at within an industry. If you are at a senior level, you need to demonstrate your awareness and understanding of the broader, more strategic elements. If you are more hands on in your role, it is worth concentrating on the more obvious issues, such as attracting more customers and keeping the orders coming in.

Do:
● Substantiate your comments with some depth of reasoning.
● Avoid giving too much detail around the economic climate and how the Government should deal with this.

Example
It is very difficult to comment on the next couple of years due to the state of the markets. However, I feel that this industry has good growth potential due to a strong customer base and the type of product will always be in demand.

What do you do to network with other professionals in the industry?

Networking can be important in many industries, but particularly in sales-based organisations. The interviewer is interested to understand who you know within the industry, how proactive you are in terms of networking and how useful you will be in potentially gaining more sales opportunities and subsequently gaining more orders.

Do:
- Describe what you do to network, such as attending conferences, trade fairs, breakfast meetings or simply phoning your contacts regularly.
- Give an example of when you have been successful in networking.
- Avoid giving a list of who you know and how you know them.

Don't:
- Give a list of meetings/clubs you belong to as you may leave the interviewer wondering if you are ever at work or always out on a jolly.

Example

I am a great advocate of 'you get out as much as you put in'; this applies to business contacts and creating opportunities. I am a member of a few business groups who meet monthly or quarterly and have developed some good contacts that have proved beneficial in terms of sales and marketing.

Who are your key contacts?

They are not specifically looking for you to detail a list of people and organisations, but trying to establish who you recognise as important contacts in your role. You may want to clarify if they mean externally in the market, or internally. It may be difficult for you to comment on specific individuals internally, but you could identify departments. For example, if you work in sales, then marketing are going to be one of your key contacts.

Example

If you are meaning contacts internally, I currently work within the sales department, taking orders and checking progress of orders for our customers. One of my most important contacts is the warehousing and despatch area. I need to stay in constant contact to understand any delivery issues that may well have a knock-on effect to our customers.

What support would you be looking for in order to perform this role?

This is an opportunity to demonstrate your understanding of the role. Before the interview try to match your own skills with that of the role and highlight any shortfalls. You may want to consider the points overleaf.

5

- Highlighting the shortfall in skills or knowledge.
- Highlighting the skills you have that will be beneficial to the role/organisation.
- The support you anticipate needing to get up to speed in the role.
- How you will take ownership of gaining support.

Don't:
- Give a long list of all the help or advice you think you will need – why on earth would they give you the job?

Example

I don't anticipate I will need much support in terms of carrying out the specific technical aspects and tasks. However, I will need someone to show me the databases and systems together with the processes you use. As soon as I start I will obviously get to know people and identify those who can help me get up to speed in specific areas.

How do you like to be rewarded in your work?

We are all different in the way we need recognition from others. Some of us are happy with a pat on the back or someone saying thank you, others seek more material reward, such as money or a gift. You could consider including the following in your responses:

- I get a real buzz when someone thanks me for what I have done.
- I really appreciate feedback and when people openly acknowledge my contribution.
- I was very appreciative when I was given an award for best sales, if a little embarrassed when I received it.

Example 1

I managed to secure the number one position in sales through sheer hard work and determination. It was nice to have this rewarded in the way of a financial bonus and most unexpected. I was particularly pleased as I was getting married that year and it meant we could have a really good honeymoon.

Example 2

I get a really strong sense of purpose and reward when someone says thank you for my contribution or hard work or pays a compliment for something I have done. This really inspires me to do more and it also encourages me to want to work with him or her again.

6 Explaining weaknesses in your CV

- ☑ Big changes
- ☑ Gaps in your CV

Big changes

There will be a variety of reasons for any weaknesses in your CV, each person's situation differing from the next. The interviewer will want to explore these reasons in some detail with you – the gaps will not necessarily be a barrier to you securing the role, but you will need to be able to explain yourself with confidence.

Describe what you have been doing since you were made redundant?

The interviewer wants to establish how you have used your time to best effect. It is important that you are able to give a clear indication of what you have been doing, whether that was job hunting or not, and how these activities have benefited you. Activities could include:

- Taking the opportunity to retrain through, for example, a training course, an occupational qualification, reading books or attending seminars.
- Undertaking unpaid or voluntary work.
- Rethinking your career options through talking to others, researching libraries and exploring websites.
- Approaching job searching as a job in itself, being very self-disciplined, creating an office at home and going to the library each day.
- Taking time out with your family.
- Fulfilling a long-held dream to travel.
- Taking on a large project, such as property improvement or purchase.
- Redecorating your own home to keep busy.
- Taking on temporary work to keep the money coming in.
- Redesigning or landscaping your garden.

Do:
- Highlight what have been the benefits from your time off, such as time for thought, refocusing on your priorities, getting fit, spending time with the family after a career of long hours or travel.

> ## TOP TIP
>
> Highlight any positive aspect of the redundancy for you, your family or your career. In particular identify anything you have learnt from having to deal with this situation that has developed you for the future. Demonstrating a positive attitude towards a negative situation demonstrates strength of character and indicates how well you deal with challenges.

6

Don't:

- Indicate that you have done nothing proactive to search for a new job.
- Indicate that you were sure 'something would come along.'
- Suggest that you are reluctant to go back to work, but that you have to for the money.

Example

I have enjoyed having a break from the commuting and travelling that I was doing in my previous job. However, I was keen not to let my motivation drop and created some structure to my job search. I set up an office area at home and have spent a number of hours each day researching companies, looking at job advertisements and searching the internet to explore my options. I have kept a file detailing which jobs I have applied for and update this regularly. Taking this approach has helped me to keep focused. I have also had some time out, getting fit and have been able to pick up my children from school most days, something that I have never been able to do before.

What have been the problems of having time away from work since being made redundant?

Be honest about what you have found difficult about being away from the workplace, this will, to some extent, indicate what is important to you about work. Problems you have encountered may include:

- Feeling 'down'.
- Missing the structure of a working environment.
- Missing the companionship of colleagues.
- Struggling to discipline yourself to job hunt.
- The worry of what will happen to you and your career.

Then focus upon describing how you have dealt with these difficulties and feelings. The interviewer wants to establish how well you have overcome them – it says a lot about you and your strength of character if you have been able to tackle these issues and view the whole situation more positively.

Example

To begin with I really missed the structure of the normal working day – getting up at a certain time and having tasks that needed to be completed. I also missed the interaction that I had on a daily basis with colleagues and customers – it gets pretty lonely on your own at home most of the day. To overcome this I have structured my day with allotted time for job search and making applications. I have then made sure that each day I have gone out and interacted with people – whether this is at interviews, seeing friends or helping out at my children's school. Taking this approach has been a big help and ensured that I have remained positive and motivated through a difficult period.

You have indicated that you were dismissed from your last role. Please describe the events that led up to this and what you have learnt from the situation.

Be factual and keep a neutral tone throughout – it is easy to become emotional, and even angry, when describing such a personal situation.

Do:
- Give a brief account of the situation.
- Identify what you have learnt from this.
- Identify how you have applied this learning since, if you have been able to.
- Be positive about the events (as much as you possibly can).
- Take some personal responsibility for what happened.

Don't:
- Give a long list of the sequence of events.
- Identify names of people involved – it is irrelevant and indiscreet.
- Be overtly critical of those involved, giving a character assassination.
- Be negative about the whole event.
- Include superfluous detail, such as, 'I said to him and he said to me.'
- Blame the other party completely.

Example
Sadly a situation that I will not forget, but it was a learning experience. When I started with the company the role I had applied for and the role I was given were two very different things. It became apparent that my team leader was struggling to complete the rotas and produce the data analysis stats for the team. They gave this to me to do. I had no idea how to tackle this and no experience of rotas or Excel spreadsheets – clearly I was going to fail. I explained the situation, but they didn't want to listen – it was a hard-nosed blame culture, and one that I realised wasn't for me. So, quite quickly, I failed in the task they had assigned me and I was asked to leave. I was really furious as I had asked for training and had enrolled myself on an evening course to try to help, but not quickly enough. I thought of suing for unfair dismissal on principle, but realised it was my word against theirs and didn't want to go through all that unpleasantness. I walked away and feel better for not being there any more.

Why have you changed jobs so frequently?

There could be very good reason for this or just be that you have a history of moving jobs regularly. Whatever the reason, you need to reassure them that you are not going to leave their employment after a few months – investing in a new employee is a costly business. You need to explain yourself with confidence and in some detail. Some of the reasons could be:

- You held a number of temporary positions while looking for the right job.
- You have struggled to settle in a particular role or organisation.
- Change in your circumstances, such as needing to move location.
- Company takeovers have led to you losing your job on more than one occasion.

Avoid:
- Stating 'I guess I have been unlucky' – you are just dismissing the question.
- Indicating you get bored quickly and like to move on.
- Indicating you don't see it as a problem, it's good to move around a lot.

Example

I took on my last two jobs because I needed the hands-on experience in this area of work, but really the work wasn't stretching me enough so I am looking to move on quickly in order to advance my career. This job appeals to me, enormously; it will challenge me more and I have now gained the necessary skills to be able to fulfil this at a competent level.

> **TOP TIP**
>
> If you have previously changed jobs frequently, offer reassurance that this is the job for you and you intend to stay – if you do!

Explaining weaknesses in your CV

Gaps in your CV

Weaknesses in your CV may include time off work due to an illness, time out from work as a carer looking after a child or other dependant, taking a more junior role, gaps in employment due to redundancy, dismissal or your previous employer going out of business. This section explores the issue of answering difficult questions that may arise from any gaps within your CV. Your CV will have done its job by getting you the interview, but be prepared to explain yourself further.

There are some gaps in your CV. Please indicate why these occurred and what you were doing during these periods of time?

There could be a variety of reasons and it is important that you are able to explain these in some detail. We would recommend you are initially brief with your explanation stating the reason and let the interviewer ask you to expand with more detail if required. Reasons for the gaps could include:

> **REMEMBER!**
>
> *Be prepared for the interviewer to ask what you have benefited from during these periods of not working.*

- You took a sabbatical.
- You went travelling – be prepared to explain where you have been. Be truthful as the interviewer may well have been there too and ask you what you thought of that country and the culture.
- You were made redundant and were job hunting.
- Raising a family – you decided to take time out until your children were school age.
- Acting as a carer for a family member who was ill.
- Studying for a qualification – change of career, retraining or to further enhance your skills in order to gain a better position within a company.

Example

I have had two periods away from work when my parents were terminally ill. I felt it was important to be the one caring for them at such a time rather than a stranger. While at home I took the opportunity to also do a distance-learning course on IT. I found this really interesting and it was good to be studying again. This has given me a greater depth of understanding around IT, which I feel will benefit me in future work.

> **TOP TIP**
>
> By voluntarily giving a short explanation of any gaps or weaknesses within your CV, or career history, at an appropriate point in the interview you are likely to reduce the interviewers' concern and therefore reduce the number of questions you get about this issue.

How much absence have you had in the last x years? What has been the reason for this?

This is a perfectly legal question and one that is very common these days. It is important to be honest as part of the company's recruitment process could be for you to undergo a medical examination, for example, if you are in the building industry or warehousing, a prerequisite for the role could be a healthy back. Also your previous company are obliged to pass on the number of days' sickness information so your version and theirs need to tally. You need to:

- Keep the information factual and to the point.
- Give a brief overview of the sickness.
- Avoid getting into lengthy detail about when you saw the doctor and what happened next.

> **REMEMBER!**
>
> *If you lie about your absences from work and you are found out, the company could withdraw the job offer.*

You have had a career break. Why do you want to come back into employment at this time?

Each person's rationale and motivation will be different. Reasons may include:

- The family are now grown up or more independent and you are needed at home less.
- You are keen to learn new skills.
- Money – be careful not to use this as your only motivator.
- You believe you have some really good skills and qualities and want to use them effectively.
- You miss the working environment and are keen to start adding value to an organisation again.
- You miss the energy you get from working with other people.

Example

Before my career break I had a responsible role that allowed me to use my technical knowledge and training to the full. Although my time away from work has been beneficial in many ways and I have enjoyed being with my family, I feel it is now time to get back into the workplace and use these skills once again and add value to an organisation.

What skills and experience did you gain during this time away from the workplace that you believe will be useful in this role?

You could have developed a range of skills and experience from undertaking a variety of activities. It is important to identify what the key skills were and

Explaining weaknesses in your CV

align them to the job you are applying for. To help do this, create a table with the skills you have obtained in one column and the skills required for the role in another (see below) – this will help you to align the skills and expand the detail further.

Don't ignore the experiences and skills you have gained outside the workplace. You may be a member of a club or social organisation and have had positions of responsibility, such as secretary of a sports club or governor at a local school. All of these roles require skills and knowledge that can be easily transferred to the workplace. In addition, they say a lot about the type of person you are.

Matching your skills to the job

Skills obtained while volunteering for a charity	Skills required for the role
● Communicate – all levels ● Worked with others within the charity	● Work within close team
● Planning and organising events	● Project management
● Marketing of events – creativity	● Use own initiative and creative approach
● Excel – data analysis	● Numeric ability, such as managing budgets
● Building relationships with suppliers	● Liaison with internal and external stakeholders

What challenges do you think you will face when you come back into the workplace?

It is important to be realistic. If you have had a period of time away from the working environment, then you are very likely to face some challenges – but each person's challenges will be different. If you don't feel that you will face any challenges, then say so but indicate why, otherwise you may come across as being unrealistic or unaware of the requirements of the role.

Do:
● Be honest.
● State clearly the challenges you think you will face.

- State how you will overcome these challenges – this gives the interviewer a good idea of your own skills/abilities and understanding of the role.
- Speak with enthusiasm about overcoming these challenges.

Don't:
- Give a long list of potential issues – the interviewer will wonder why you are applying and how well you are suited for the role.
- Sound as if the whole job will overface you.

Example

I am sure there will be a number of challenges. I guess, initially, a challenge will be getting to know everyone in the team/department and understanding their roles and responsibilities; however, I don't see this as a huge problem. I am personable and open in my approach and not afraid to ask lots of questions. Also getting used to different systems and processes will be a challenge. I am a quick learner, though, and able to pick up new things quickly.

What are you looking forward to as part of being back at work?

It needs to be more of a response than 'the money' or 'the pension'. You don't have to go into great detail, but some reasons could be:

- Being part of a team.
- Using my skills and knowledge.
- Bouncing ideas off others.
- Doing something worthwhile.
- Contributing to projects or tasks.
- Using my thinking ability.
- Using my brain again.
- Having others challenge me.
- Learning new skills and developing my experience.
- Some financial security for my family.

Example

I am really looking forward to being part of a team again where I feel I can contribute and add value. I am eager to have my creativity and thinking stimulated and challenged by other people. Coupled with this it will be good to be able to make decisions that are meaningful and make a difference. Oh – and the money!

> **TOP TIP**
>
> Avoid indicating that if it were your choice you wouldn't be going back to work at all.

Why do you think you were out of work for so long?

A challenging question, so stick to the main facts and avoid giving detail that isn't really needed. There can be a variety of reasons. These could include:

- Your own choice – you had received a redundancy payment and could afford to stay off work for a while.
- Your CV was not up to scratch and you found it difficult to get interviews. You have now changed this to reflect your skills and experiences better.
- Your interview technique was not as good as it could be – you have now received some advice on this.
- You were unrealistic about the kind of position you could obtain.
- You deliberately took your time looking around to make sure you got the right job with the right company.
- You were in a time of transition in your personal life and not sure of your permanent location.
- High unemployment in the area you live or work in.
- A lot of people with similar skills to you job hunting.
- Limited vacancies advertised.

Other reasons may have been more to do with your motivation, skill set or keenness to look for promotion rather than a job at the same level. Whatever the reason, state it clearly in your answer and also try to include the following:

- If you took time out, describe what you have been doing in that time to keep busy or develop your skills.
- If you think the reason was to do with your application or interview technique, then say what you have done to improve this.
- Speak knowledgeably about the local job market that has affected you and what you have done to try to overcome this limiting factor.

Don't:
- Use excuses about the job market that are not true, you will be found out.
- Speak with despair about the situation indicating you have given up hope of ever finding work.

Example
I realise it looks like I have been out of work for some time but I have tried to use this time effectively and obtain new skills by doing some courses. I became aware that my CV wasn't very good and didn't really reflect my experiences and achievements, so I got someone to help me with it. I have also sought advice on how to improve my interview skills – I hope it shows!

How long have you been looking for a job?

You may have only just started your job search, or it could be that you have been looking for some time. You could have been on the hunt for something different since you started your last job, but do you really want to tell them that? Whatever the answer, give some indication of why you are looking as well as how long for.

Do:
- Give an approximate indication of how long you have been looking for a new job.
- Indicate your particular interest in their vacancy and explain why you are interested.

Don't:
- Indicate that it seems like a lifetime.
- Suggest that you have applied for hundreds of jobs.
- Blame your lack of success solely on market conditions or the area that you live in.
- Appear resigned to another rejection before you even get started on the interview.

Example

I recognised there was a down turn in sales at my current employer and it seemed inevitable that some job losses would occur as a result. So I started tentatively looking a couple of months ago to see what options are available to me. I also felt it was a good idea to seek out new job opportunities and see this as a good chance to make a change.

After such a long career break you must be out of touch with what has gone on in the industry and the changes that have taken place?

You need to overcome the interviewer's assumption that just because you haven't been in the workplace doesn't mean that you have taken no interest in what has been going on. Actions you may have taken could include:

- Keeping up to date through reading trade journals, newspapers and talking to ex-colleagues.

REMEMBER!

Avoid going into the interview feeling negative about the fact there are gaps in your CV, this will come across in your answers and may only lead the interviewer to question how positive a person you are and your suitability for the job.

- Recently getting back up to speed knowing that you would be job hunting.
- Undertaking some distance learning to develop your knowledge further.

Do:
- Indicate that you were aware that this was a danger of being away from work so you took some actions to ensure it didn't happen.
- State clearly the actions you have taken, and why you took them.
- Summarise what you see as the most significant current issues in the industry and what the key changes have been since you were last working.

Don't:
- Dismiss the interviewer's concern or say, 'I'm sure I will soon pick it up.'
- Indicate that you have been so busy as a carer/parent/travelling that you have no idea what has gone on.
- Indicate you needed some time out so have purposefully stepped back from it all.

Example

I have been away from the workplace for about 18 months and, of course, lots of things have happened in the commercial world to affect this industry. Obviously I kept up to date generally through listening to the news, but in the last couple of months I have got back into reading the trade journal and also chatting to people I used to work with. I think the key challenges now are ensuring that the business is as cost effective as possible as profit margins are so tight.

 Fitting in

- ☑ Your personality
- ☑ Your attitude to work
- ☑ You and the new job
- ☑ Working with colleagues
- ☑ Practicalities
- ☑ Some strange questions

Your personality

This section is all about you! It focuses on how best to sell your skills, experience and knowledge effectively. It is important that you do this and use examples that best explain your style and personality. Let your personality shine through.

Tell me about yourself

The difficulty with this question is where to start – it allows you to talk about all aspects of your life, career, skills and qualities.

Do:
- Give a brief overview of yourself.
- Stick to facts, such as a snap shot of your career to date.
- How you have got to where you are today in terms of your career.
- Substantiate the facts. If you tell them you like watching films or reading books expect to expand on this further – they may well be a film/book buff themselves.
- Include information about what you do outside of work – sports, member of a club, reading, music.

Don't:
- Go into minute detail around where you went to school, what subjects you took or what type of house you live in.

Example

I left university, went travelling for a year and then undertook a number of temporary jobs before securing my current role as an adviser. I am now looking for a bigger challenge to enhance my skills further and develop my career.

> **Panasonic's perfect candidate is a punctual, well-presented individual who is able to demonstrate confidence while retaining a degree of humility. They should have taken the initiative to research the company, be able to identify with the company culture and have some pre-prepared relevant questions for the interviewer that show signs of enthusiasm for the role.**
>
> EMMA BOYLE, HR ASSISTANT, PANASONIC

How would you describe yourself?

This is your opportunity for a sales pitch – a quick one-minute précis of your
skills and attributes. In your answer:

Do:
- Align your skills to the role and the organisation. Use some of the words
  they have used to describe the job; for example, team values, ethics, strategic,
  initiative, innovative, organised.
- Keep it brief and to the point.
- Use powerful and positive words – 'I am', 'I will', 'I have'.

Don't:
- Use words such as 'hope', 'think' and 'would like'.

Example

*I am a strong communicator at all levels and enjoy working within a changing organisation.
I rise to a challenge and thrive on delivering against deadlines while working on my own
initiative. I have a strong work ethic and a willingness to learn and take on extra responsibility.*

How would your friends describe you?

Be careful here – because it is a friend's opinion they are asking for, don't lose
focus on where you are, this is a job interview. You may also want to inject a
little humour. You could use descriptions such as confidential, reliable, good
fun, enthusiastic and a great cook!

   This question is about the interviewer finding out what type of person you
are and how well you know yourself, so don't feel that you have to be critical
of yourself.

Example

*I think my friends would say that I am a good listener and will offer honest advice and
feedback, even if it isn't what they want to hear. I have helped a number of friends work
through what it is they want to do for a career and feel I have been useful in doing this because
of the breadth of my own work experience and open approach.*

What are your key strengths and how have you used them?

They want to find out if you have a good understanding of your own skills
and qualities and how you make best use of them. They will be interested
to see if you can relate your strengths to the skills and qualities required in
their vacancy.

Fitting in

Do:

- Provide a short list of your strengths in order to create a positive impression of yourself.
- Give a short example of how you use your strengths.
- Relate your strengths to the role you are being interviewed for.
- Use positive language – 'I am', 'I do'.

Don't:

- Provide an endless list, you need to keep it punchy.
- Make a statement that you cannot justify or provide an example to illustrate.
- Describe qualities or skills that are not work related – for example, a good pool player, chess player or swimmer.

Example

My strengths are my team working skills – I work effectively with my colleagues and offer them support to complete work. I have very good attention to detail being thorough in checking facts when reconciling bank statements. I am keen to please customers and I always take the time to understand how I can help them and check to make sure I have done what they wanted me to.

What are your weaknesses/development needs?

They want to find out if you have a good understanding of your own shortfalls and if you have already taken any action to develop these. You need to:

- Describe an upside for every weakness; for example, 'I am quite an impulsive person, but this is because I am so keen to get on with things and really enjoy my work.'
- Describe the actions you have taken to overcome these weaknesses/ development needs.
- Identify any specific things you would have to learn if you got the job – this shows you understand what they are looking for.

Don't:

- Provide an endless list – why on earth would they then give you the job?
- Make a statement that you cannot justify or provide an example to illustrate.

Example

My development needs are my organisational skills – I have worked to overcome this by doing a daily 'To Do list', which means that I keep track of things. My other weakness is my tendency to forget that not all my colleagues have as much experience as me and therefore sometimes take longer to complete tasks. Rather than get irritated with them I make sure that I offer them help and assistance wherever possible.

Would you describe yourself as a leader or follower?

You may well do both and it depends on the situation – if that is the case, then state it. Be prepared to follow this up with a more detailed explanation and refer to work or leisure situations.

Example

It would depend on the situation I was in. I would like to think that I could take on either role. For instance, with my football team I am one of the most experienced players and have been with the club for some years. I am looked upon to take the lead and am very comfortable doing this, using my knowledge and expertise to help encourage and support others. At work I would generally take on a team member role as we already have a leader within our department. However, I have, on a couple of occasions, deputised for him in his absence – but I don't have a need to be the boss all of the time.

What outside interests do you have?

The interviewer could be breaking the ice with this question or wanting to establish what type of person you are by understanding how you spend your spare time. Consider the following:

- If you tend to have more solitary pursuits, you may be quite an introverted person, or it could be that you have a very busy and responsible job and want some chill out time.
- If you enjoy hectic pastimes involving the company of others, you could be very extroverted or you have a sedentary and solitary job and you like to get out and talk with people. Whatever it is:

Do:
- Highlight your key interests/hobbies.
- Link these to your job if possible.
- Identify what you have learnt; for example, as chair of a society you have to lead others, something that you haven't done at work, but you are developing skills in this area.
- Expand on what you get out of these activities – keeping fit, time to reflect alone or enjoying the company of others.

Fitting in

Don't:
- Give a long list of things you like to do that, realistically, no one could enjoy along with a full-time job.
- Give lots of detail; for instance, what position you play at hockey and where your club is – it can be very boring and they may just be being polite by asking.
- Extend the truth – if you haven't been to the gym for four months it may show.

Example

I do a variety of sports but predominantly I run three times a week and play tennis for a local club. I am able to use my experience as an ex-county player and offer coaching and support to the other players. I captain the team and this enables me to use my leadership skills, giving direction and focus. I also enjoy cooking and reading.

What do you do to switch off from work?

There is no right or wrong answer as we are all different. Some of us like to switch off by expelling energy, by thrashing around a tennis court or pounding the tarmac. Alternatively, you may like to retreat to the comfort of your sofa with a good book and a glass of wine.

Do:
- Be honest. If you mention you read a lot, then you may be asked who is your favourite author.
- Be brief and stick to the facts.

Don't:
- Give a long list of things you do.
- Give specific detail about which soap operas you watch and who your favourite character is – it's not necessary.

Example

I am the kind of person who needs to exercise to switch off and expel some energy. This also gives me the opportunity to think about things. However, if I am really tired, then a good film and a glass of wine in the comfort of my own home is perfect.

Do you enjoy routine tasks?

Some of us draw comfort from having an element of routine in our work and others find it quite suffocating. You need to consider the points opposite.

- Familiarise yourself with the job description. If you enjoy routine tasks, then say so and state why; for example, 'I like to know my tasks well, I am organised and systematic, I am structured in the way that I work.'
- If there are lots of routine tasks mentioned, then avoid saying that it frustrates you – why would you be applying?

Example

I have to say that I wouldn't want to be undertaking routine tasks all of the time. However, I do have an appreciation that these need to be completed as it is important for the team and the department.

How creative are you?

You may not need to be creative in your role and hence use this skill infrequently. You may be a budding artist in your spare time, so you could talk about that. You could approach this question:

- By qualifying if they mean being creative at work.
- By asking what they mean by being creative.
- By saying, 'Not at work, but I really enjoy handicraft hobbies, which allow me to express my creativity.'
- Some examples you could consider talking about would be: a new marketing display stand, company brochure, team building event or a company presentation.

Avoid saying:
- 'No, I don't like all that fluffy arty stuff.'
- 'Not a creative bone in my body.'
- 'Didn't know I was applying to be an artist.'

> **REMEMBER!**
>
> *If you are applying to be a graphic designer, web designer or marketer, then be ready to have a portfolio of your work with you.*

Give me an example of when you have been creative?

They want to find out about your thought processes and perhaps what you consider to be creativity. It could be they are looking for you to describe something innovative or how you have designed a new product. You may want to question what they mean. Include the following in your example:

- What the situation was.
- Why this needed a creative approach.
- In what way you were creative.

- How successful you feel you were.
- What feedback you received.

Tell me about a current world issue that interests you.

This question may be one to break the ice, to assess your interests in current affairs or to see how in touch/interested you are in this area. If you are applying for a position that has a strong link to current affairs issues, then have a detailed answer ready together with a rationale as to why this is of particular interest.

Do:
- Have an example ready that demonstrates your understanding.
- Give specific facts.
- Avoid giving your opinion about potentially sensitive specific subjects.

What is the most challenging thing you have ever done outside of work?

The interviewer may be genuinely interested to see what other interests you have and what you consider to be a challenge and why. The type of challenge you take on can also say a lot about you as an individual. They could be using this as an icebreaking question. You may want to:

- Consider the range of activities that you are involved in.
- Describe what it was, how you completed this and why it was so challenging to you.
- Describe what you got out of the experience and how you felt.

Some example areas you could use span from sailing the Atlantic to completing your GCSE maths while working. The list is endless and the rationale for completion is personal.

Example

I had always wanted to complete the London half marathon, a challenge I had set myself to do before I was 40 years old. It was the training that was difficult, more in terms of trying to fit it in with work, family commitments and daylight hours. I took advice from others and devised a training plan and stuck to this as much as possible. It was so challenging as I had previously only run much shorter distances, but I was also motivated to raise money for a charity that I am very passionate about. When I completed it, I felt great and more confident in myself, realising how lucky I was to take part in such an event.

How do you achieve a good work/life balance?

Companies are placing more and more emphasis on encouraging their staff to have a good balance in their lives. Responses you could give are:

- Have lunch outside of the office rather than sitting at your desk.
- Home working on a specific day(s) of the week in order to cut down on commuting time.
- Work a four-and-a-half day week or nine-day fortnight.
- Walk or cycle to work as it's both quicker and it provides exercise and fresh air.
- Attend the gym during my lunchtime.
- Leave on time at least twice a week.

Example

This is really quite important to me as I am very keen on sports and keeping fit, which helps me relax and switch off from work. I therefore make sure I leave work on time at least twice a week so I can go to the gym for a run when I get home. I avoid, where possible, taking work home at weekends although sometimes it is necessary during the week and I may well spend my commute time reading information, but everyone needs 'me time' and time off.

Give an example when your trust in others has been misplaced

The interviewer is looking for you to talk about a specific situation to establish predominantly what it was, how it came about and what you learnt from it so that it doesn't happen again. For example, it could be a situation where you trusted a colleague with a piece of confidential information only to have this confidence broken. Consider addressing the following:

- What the situation was.
- Why you placed your trust in this person.
- How you realised that your trust had been misplaced.
- How you addressed this with your colleague.
- What you learnt from this experience.
- How will you ensure it doesn't happen again.

Example

I was managing the collation of the performance pay reviews and another manager within the department asked me what the outcome had been for a particular employee. Although she had not directly been involved in the collation of the data, she was party to confidential employee information, so I shared this detail with that manager. Unfortunately, during a heated debate she was having with the member of staff, the manager gave out this piece of information, which she should not have done – she was mortified, but the damage had been done. It was a hard lesson, but one that has stayed with me.

What one aspect of yourself would you change and why?

The interviewer is looking to establish how well you know yourself, your skills and shortfalls. Similar to strengths and weaknesses it is important to be able to identify the positive aspects of a potentially negative quality.

Example

I get very engrossed in my work and tend to work long hours as a result, I just don't notice the time pass. Sometimes this can be a problem as I don't get away from work early enough to spend time with my family. I now set an alarm on my watch to let me know when I should be leaving the office and have found this a good prompt to make me pack up and get going.

Who has been the biggest influence on your life and why?

This is a general question that helps the interviewer get to know you a bit and help you to warm up to answering more work-based questions. Answers will vary from family members to teachers, friends or even famous people. Include in your answer:

- Who the person is.
- How he or she has influenced your life.
- What benefits there have been for you.
- What learning you have taken from this.

Don't:

- Talk at great length.
- Go into minute detail as to how that person has influenced your life.

Example

Other than obviously my parents, the biggest influence on my life was my drama teacher at school. She was the first person to identify that I was allowing my shyness to get in the way of interacting more widely with pupils and staff and stopping me joining in some of the many after school clubs that were available. She taught me a few techniques to overcome this shyness and assured me that once I got used to using them they would actually make me feel more confident meeting new people – she was right.

Who has been the biggest influence in your career and why?

This is likely to be a colleague, manager or member of staff and probably someone who helped you learn a really important lesson or developed your skills in a particular way. The interviewer will be interested to hear:

● Who the person is.
● How he or she influenced you.
● Why this person has had such a big impact upon you.
● How this person has impacted upon your career.

Example

The biggest influence upon my career to date has been a manager I had a few years ago. He was really supportive, but also challenging in his approach – always pushing me to achieve more and do new things at work. He had an open door policy and I felt I could chat things through with him whenever I needed. He also had really high standards so I knew whatever work I did had to be good. I have a lot to be thankful to him for – he was a big factor in me achieving the success I have had and set me a good example as to how to manage my own team.

What is the most significant thing you have learnt from your career so far?

The interviewer wants to find out as much information about you as a person as possible and this includes what you have learnt and how you use this learning. The interviewer is looking for a specific example, one that may have transformed your learning or maybe given you the 'light bulb' moment. Consider the following:

● What the situation was.
● Why this was such a big deal.
● What the learning actually was.
● How you have used this learning effectively since.

Example

Some years ago I was made redundant from my job as a sales clerk and forced to consider my career, where I wanted to go and what I wanted to do. I realised that I really enjoyed taking time out and exercising, finding the change in my fitness fascinating and I feel so much better physically. This prompted me to look into furthering my knowledge and skills within the fitness area and hence why I am where I am today in my chosen career – I get satisfaction from educating others and keeping fit and healthy.

Fitting in

Your attitude to work

Potential employers are always keen to explore a candidates' attitude towards work, what they find motivating, stressful or challenging. This section identifies a range of typical questions you may be asked about these areas.

••

What is the most challenging situation you have faced at work?

You need to give a specific example of what this was and include:

- How you dealt with the challenge.
- What your approach was to overcoming this.
- How and why you did what you did.

Do:

- Focus on an example that had a positive outcome for you.
- Take the opportunity to send positive messages to the interviewer about yourself and the qualities you have to deal with situations like this.
- Consider using situations such as redundancy, disciplinary, company restructure or difficult targets as they can be challenging and cover a range of skills.

Example

Due to continued poor performance of one of my staff members I was in the position of having to dismiss her. I had carried out all of the relevant meetings leading up to this and was faced with the final decision. I had consulted with the relevant parties, for example HR and my manager. I ensured I had all of the details available and invited the member of staff concerned into a meeting. After delivering all of the necessary information I asked her for her comments. Although initially she was very angry about this, she eventually accepted the decision. It was challenging because it was a difficult decision affecting someone's livelihood; however, the business and my team could not support this person. I learnt to remain detached emotionally and found that researching the facts and talking this through with my manager helped me a great deal.

What do you dislike about your current job?

In order to present a positive image of yourself, your answer needs to:

- Be factually based.
- Concentrate on one element of your job.
- Explain why you don't like this aspect of your work.
- Explain how you deal with this part of your job.

Don't:

- Detail a long list of things you don't like.
- Include tasks that will be found in this new role.

Example

I dislike some of the more routine paper-based tasks and, as a result, have tried to reduce some of them by creating electronic versions. However, there is still an element of the work that needs to be undertaken with pen and paper. I ensure I do these tasks on a regular basis and keep on top of them rather than leaving them until last. I appreciate the importance of these tasks and the information they produce for colleagues.

What do you like about your current job?

Include a variety of tasks or aspects of the job. For example, if you work in customer services and enjoy meeting and talking with customers and building relationships, ensure you back this up with how you achieve the sale and meet the customer's needs. Expect to answer follow-on questions that focus on a specific occasion when you have done this.

Example

I really enjoy the challenge of solving a problem. I liked to use all of my analysis skills, liaise with others, research the internet, read publications and then piece all of this information together in order to resolve an issue or make a recommendation. To then see this implemented is really rewarding.

How do you handle pressure in the workplace?

How you handle pressure most likely depends on where it is coming from. Is it self-inflicted or out of your control? You can approach this question in a number of different ways:

- You prefer to have an organised and systematic approach in order to alleviate any pressures.
- You are aware of priorities and able to identify which urgent or important tasks need priority status.
- You challenge people back – if they are insisting on reducing timescales, you question further as to when, and if, it is urgently required.
- You take time out to reorganise yourself.
- You negotiate on timescales and priorities.
- You like to seek assistance and talk things through with colleagues and your manager.

Fitting in

Don't say:

- You get really stressed and let everyone know how you are feeling.
- You lose your temper and then everyone leaves you alone.
- You take time off sick, you just can't cope.

Do you like working under pressure?

This is likely to require more than a yes or no answer. Be prepared to give some rationale as to why you do or don't like pressure – we are all different.

Example 1: if you like working under pressure

It depends where the pressure is coming from. If we are nearing the end of a project and the final elements need to be completed, then, yes, I find this quite enjoyable in terms of pressure – it helps me energise and keeps me focused.

Example 2: if you don't like working under pressure

If I am in a situation where other people have left tasks until the last minute through their own disorganised approach and then involve me, I can feel a little frustrated. Of course I help out, but the situation could have been avoided or made much simpler if they had only asked earlier.

What situations do you find stressful in the workplace?

You need to:

- State exactly what you find stressful and how you address or manage this.
- Be honest – you may be found out once in the post.
- Ensure you fully understand the job you have applied for. You don't want to give a list of things you find stressful only to find they are incorporated in the job description.

Example

I particularly stress about giving presentations to large audiences. I have addressed this through training and mentoring from my manager and peers, however, this still doesn't stop me worrying about it. I am able to deliver and have received some very good feedback, but half-an-hour before I deliver a presentation I need some time to focus.

How do you ensure that you are professional in your behaviour?

What the interviewer wants to assess is if you can identify the importance of being professional and the impact on your reputation if you are not. Aspects to include are listed opposite.

- The work standards you set yourself.
- How you interact with colleagues and customers.
- Why you think it is important to be professional.

Example

I try to remain professional in everything I do at work. I respect the views and contributions of others. I recognise the need to ensure I use the right language at work and am considerate and interested in what people do. I have strong business awareness and I always make sure my appearance is appropriate; for example, if I have a client visit, then I adopt a more formal dress code. I also ensure that I don't make inappropriate comments with customers, even if they are lacking in professionalism themselves.

How do you maintain interest in your work?

They want to establish how easily you are distracted from tasks or, indeed, where your interests and motivators are while you are at work. It is important to sound upbeat and enthusiastic. You may want to consider:

- Outlining some of the more enjoyable aspects of your work.
- Identify the different resources you have, such as internet, customers, databases, materials and interactions with people.

Example

Any job has aspects that are more interesting and enjoyable than others. However, I find having a variety of tasks to undertake keeps my interest and my focus on the job. I enjoy the interaction I have with customers and my colleagues and this offsets some of the more routine tasks I have to carry out.

What do you get enthusiastic about at work?

This will vary dramatically from one person to another and there really isn't a right or wrong answer. The interviewer wants to understand a little more about what makes you tick and what you are likely to enjoy at work. Include in your answer:

- A brief summary of things you get enthusiastic about at work.
- Why you enjoy those things so much.

Don't:
- List everything you do.
- Show no enthusiasm for anything at all.

Fitting in

Example

I get really enthusiastic about new products at work, I just love learning all about them, helping my colleagues to understand them and then explaining to customers what they are all about and how they might be beneficial for them. I also enjoy seeing the sales go up as we all become more confident in dealing with these new products

How do you go about prioritising your work?

You need to:

- Clearly state that you identify urgent and important tasks and decide what the impact is on others.
- Talk about the systems or tools you use, such as a diary, project plan or lists.
- Describe a typical day or perhaps a project you have completed recently to illustrate your approach.

Don't:

- Say, 'It just happens' or 'I do this all the time.'

Example

The work I do is generally very time pressured and I can only plan and prioritise on the day or, if I am lucky, the night before. I identify which tasks I know are important and those that are urgent and put these to the top of the pile. I also recognise that what I do impacts on the work of others, so if I fail to prioritise, this can escalate further. If I recognise a conflict in terms of my time and ability to meet deadlines, I speak with others in the team who can help, or liaise and negotiate with my manager.

What is the most useful piece of feedback you have ever been given in the workplace?

The interviewer wants to assess how well you listen to others and take on board information. This could be feedback that is potentially hurtful and demotivating or perhaps insightful and useful.

Do give an example that:

- You can give some depth of detail to.
- You have taken action on the feedback.
- Has been useful to you in your role.
- Helped develop you in some way.
- Has a positive outcome.

Don't give an example:
- Where someone was overly critical.
- That was subjective or unconstructive.
- That you didn't do anything with.

Example

I was once told that I focus on the implementation and practical elements of a project, and am too keen to get started rather than consider the wider issues and the bigger picture – sometimes missing out on key links in information. I respected this person's view as he was a successful manager. He gave me some advice and since then I have tried hard to ensure I take my time, talk with others and look at the whole situation properly rather than getting started on the work too quickly.

What would you consider to be a good work environment?

The interviewer is not interested in whether you would like blue or grey walls but in the kind of things that are important to you in the workplace. In your answer:

- Ensure you are constructive and focus on practical elements.
- It may be important for you to have a shower, kitchen area or gym at work, but be careful not to sound too focused just on what 'I want' but consider what is good for others as well.
- Use examples such as, 'I like working in an open-plan environment as this encourages teamwork', or, 'I am very aware of health and safety issues and believe it is important that facilities need to be clean and tidy.'

Example

I enjoy working in an open-plan environment. This encourages the sharing of ideas and I get energy and buzz from being with other people. However, when necessary, it is also useful to be able to have a quiet area where I can have thinking time or perhaps be more creative.

TOP TIP

Whatever your preference for a working environment, it is important to be able to give some rationale behind why that is the case.

Describe an occasion when you have taken a calculated risk at work. Why did you do this?

The interviewer is trying to establish if you are willing to push boundaries and to what extent – is this for the benefit of the team/organisation or to make you look good? Choose an example where the risk paid off. You need to include the detail suggested overleaf.

Fitting in

- What the situation was.
- What the risk involved was.
- How you assessed the risk.
- What the benefits of taking this risk were.
- If you would you do it again.

Example

I was involved in developing and launching a new product at work. It was an untested market for us, but one that others had had some success in. I did some research on potential revenue that could be created and weighed this up against the cost of developing and launching the product. I recommended to the Board that we go ahead with the idea and predicted a payback within two years. I identified the risks to them and suggested some ways we could minimise these. They were happy to go ahead and I am pleased to say it is now one of our best selling products and has paid for itself many times over.

How would you evaluate your last boss?

There is nothing worse than someone coming for an interview and then just criticising his or her boss – if that is what you are saying about that person, what will you end up saying about your new boss or colleagues? It is also extremely unprofessional. If you think your current employer is a 'dragon' or has a self-inflated ego, then keep those thoughts to yourself and think of something constructive to say.

TOP TIP

Keep evaluations of your last boss brief – don't get into long descriptions of your boss's strengths and weaknesses, it is you who is being interviewed, not your boss.

Example

My boss understands her role very well and plays an important part in setting the strategy for the company. She has offered some good advice to me since I have been there.

You and the new job

This section is focused on the specific job you have applied for. It is important that you are able to demonstrate your understanding of the role and how your skills and experiences align to this. Also, be prepared to answer any questions relating to where your development areas may be.

How have you prepared for this interview?

The interviewer can tell a lot about you by the way you answer this question. Are you someone who plans and organises well in advance or are you a last minute sort of person? Consider highlighting some of the following actions:

- Read the website.
- Received some company brochures.
- Prepared and highlighted my key skills and achievements (you may have notes with you to back this up).
- Familiarised myself with the company culture.
- Spoken to a friend who works here.
- Familiarised myself with the job description.

REMEMBER!

You need to substantiate any statements you make about your preparation. If you have read the website, ensure you can make a meaningful comment about it.

Why do you want this job?

This is your chance to do demonstrate that you really understand the job and are the best person for it.

Do:
- State clearly why you want the job.
- Align your skills to the job, explaining why you would be good at it.
- Keep it short and snappy.

Don't:
- Sound like you are doing them a favour by being there.
- Use passive language such as 'I think' or 'I hope'.

Example

I am really interested in your company as it has such a good reputation in the market. I have the relevant skills and attributes to undertake the role, such as strong project management, planning and organising, and good communication skills. I thrive on a challenge and enjoy working within a team. I am passionate about delivering quality customer service.

Fitting in

What interests you least about this job?

Identify just one or two things that you can highlight and turn into something positive. It could be that you dislike recording time sheets, invoicing, or tying up paperwork.

Do:
- Keep it brief.
- Mention only one or two minor points.
- Turn these into a positive; for example, you appreciate these things have to be done as they are important to the business.

Don't:
- Give a long list and leave them wondering why you have bothered to come to the interview.
- Say, 'I don't really know, I haven't really thought about it' – of course you have!

Example

I guess filing is not something that interests me greatly, or other people, I am sure. However, I recognise the importance of ensuring this is kept up to date and it is something that I do on a regular basis as I really dislike it getting out of hand and what should be a five-minute job turning into a huge ordeal if it is left too long.

How long do you think you will stay with us?

The interviewer wants to know if you are reliable – the company is not going to invest in someone if they think you are a 'fly by night' who will leave after five minutes in the job. You need to consider this question carefully if you have moved jobs regularly and explain why this has been the case (see the next question). If not, then you need to persuade the interviewer that you are planning on being there for a considerable time – enough time for the company to get a return on their investment.

It is impossible to state exactly how long you would stay with any employer, who knows what may happen to you or the company.

Don't:
- Try to be clever and say things like, 'Hard to say, what do you think?' You are avoiding the question.
- Think that saying, 'I want a job for life', will necessarily be seen as a positive response by all employers. They may like to have fresh minds in the business every few years.

Example

I would like to think that I am a reliable member of any workforce. I am really excited by this position and your company, so I would like to think I would be around for the foreseeable future. I am looking to be able to enhance my skills and knowledge and add value.

You have been with your current employer such a short time, why are you looking for a move so soon?

The concern the organisation has is that if they go to the expense of employing and training you, are you going to leave them quickly too? You need to be able to persuade the interviewer that this isn't the case. There could be all sorts of reasons why you have made the choice to move on so quickly:

- Redundancy.
- Hours of travel more than anticipated.
- Job content not as advertised.
- Temporary position.

Whatever the reasons were, explain them in a positive, upbeat manner – it was a learning experience for you.

Example

I realise it may look like I am moving very quickly. However, the content of the role I am undertaking currently is not as advertised and it is not providing the challenges that I anticipated and expected. I am disappointed as the company is doing well and the people I am working with are very nice, but I need to be pushed more.

Does this job fit in with your career plan?

If it does, then this is an easy question to answer – just indicate how it fits and what skills and experience you think you will gain from it that will be useful for the future. If it doesn't, then don't:

- State simply that it doesn't.
- Suggest that it is just a stop gap; unless it is a temporary job, no employer wants to hear that.

Include in your answer some indication of how you feel you will benefit from having this job – such as skills you will learn, understanding a new industry, working with different customers.

Example

This role will give me a good appreciation of the manufacturing industry, one that I haven't worked in before, while at the same time allowing me to further develop my sales skills and work in a larger team. These are all useful skills that can only be of benefit in developing me for the future.

You have been a long time with your current employer, how do you think you will cope with the change?

It is never going to be easy changing job, so don't play it down completely. If you say you are excited by the challenge – sound it! If you say you have some concerns and are worried about it, indicate how you will cope with these.

Example

I have already considered this and I am really excited about a new job and working environment. I realise there is a lot to learn, but that will be part of the challenge and something I will really enjoy. I am keen to get into the role as quickly as possible and recognise I am going to need the experience and knowledge of those people I will be working with to help me through the early weeks.

Why do you want to leave your present employment?

It is important that you paint a positive picture of what may be a negative situation. If you hate your boss or the people you work with, you need to find a way of describing this in a positive light – or think of another reason. There are a variety of reasons that may have prompted you to move jobs, including:

- Need more of a challenge.
- Issues with the company culture.
- Commute is too long.
- Looking for more travel.
- Looking for less travel.
- Want more responsibility.
- Career change.

> **REMEMBER!**
>
> *If you are going to use an example like the one below, make sure the role you are applying for does not include travel too.*

Example

I have a young family and I am currently away from home two or three nights a week, which is proving a challenge for all of us. As much as I enjoy the work I am doing, this is impacting on my work/life balance. I am very happy to travel, but I need to keep the level of this in control for myself and my family.

Working with colleagues

Be prepared to answer questions that focus on how others see you and your style when working with colleagues. The interviewer is keen to establish how well you know yourself and understand your strengths and development needs.

....

What would your current manager say is your biggest strength?

Be realistic in your answer because the interviewer may ask your current employer for a reference. Rather than going into great amounts of detail, stick to basic adjectives and specific tasks you have completed well. You could use some of the following:

- Good communicator.
- Focused in approach.
- Organised and systematic.
- Creative and innovative.
- Reliable.
- Willing to challenge.
- Excellent project manager.
- Sales drive.
- Good team player.

What would your manager say is your biggest fault?

The trick here is to turn a fault or negative into a positive quality.

Example 1

They would probably say I am too helpful. I tend to take on too much as I am keen to learn and develop and there have been a couple of times when I struggled to meet a deadline because of this.

Example 2

They would probably say I was too organised, leaving little room for changing priorities. I have always delivered against timescales, but need to sit back and refocus if things change.

What would your colleagues say is your biggest strength?

Stick to the facts and be realistic. No colleague is going to say you are the best thing since sliced bread, but they could say any of the things overleaf.

Fitting in

- Trustworthy.
- Supportive.
- Encouraging.
- Reliable.
- Willing to help.
- Calm in a crisis.
- Organised.
- Structured.
- Flexible.
- Good team player.

What would your colleagues say is your biggest fault?

Remain focused on giving a brief description. You may want to turn this into a light-hearted example or take a more serious approach.

Example 1

They would probably say I am really particular with my filing and get irritated if people put things away in the wrong place. They tend to tease me about this and sometimes run around putting stuff away when I come in the office.

Example 2

I am very detail conscious and some of them get annoyed about my dotting 'I's and crossing 'T's as they are more innovative than me and less concerned with accuracy.

What kinds of people do you enjoy working with?

As much as some people are 'a laugh' or 'good fun', try to focus on skills relating to work. In your answer:

- Identify some of the people you have enjoyed working with.
- Highlight their strengths and why you enjoyed working with them.

Example

I thrive on working with people who I can learn from and who have a different skill set to my own. I enjoy people who will challenge my thinking and force me to consider ideas that do not come to me naturally.

What kinds of people do you find it more difficult to work with and how have you gone about working with them?

In answering this question:

- Consider both parts of the question.
- Explain why there are certain people you haven't enjoyed working with.
- Be as constructive as possible, recognising the positive in the situation.
- Identify anything you learnt from working with these individuals.

Don't:
Give a long list of the types of people who have irritated you in the past.

Example
I can get frustrated with lazy or unenthusiastic people as this can have a detrimental effect on the team and the work we are doing. I realise that not everyone is as focused and interested in their work as others, but it can have a big impact on the team as a whole. I once worked with someone who was not interested in a project we were doing. I asked him what his concerns were and discovered he had been allocated some pretty mundane tasks. We agreed to share the workload, giving him a more creative role, playing to his strengths. The end result was that he was far more enthusiastic and ended up playing a major role in the delivery.

Do you prefer working alone or with other people?

In answering this question:

- You need to be truthful.
- Be prepared to expand on what you have said and explain why.
- If you do enjoy working with others, describe the benefits of this.
- If you don't enjoy working with others, then indicate why.

Example
It depends on what I am doing. I enjoy the buzz and energy from being with other people, bouncing ideas and gathering thoughts, as this is important for me to fulfil my work in the marketing department. However, there are also times where I find working on my own very useful as I am able to think more clearly without interruption.

Fitting in

WARNING!

Consider the role you are applying for. There is no point applying for a role that is not going to suit your personality or working style preferences. If the role is team based and constantly requires you to liaise and work with others, then be careful not to describe yourself as someone who needs to work on your own.

When working as part of a team what role do you typically take?

This could be dependent upon the people you are working with or the kind of task you are working on. Your style may be flexible and, if so, it is important to stress this. In addition, are you someone who sometimes takes charge, gets on with the work, supports your colleagues, thinks of good ideas or liaises well with other people?

Refer to the Belbin team roles on page 245 for a list and description of different team roles, which may help you categorise you own role and preferred style of working in a team.

Example

It all depends on the situation and who I am working with. I am a member of an amateur dramatic society outside of work and I take on the role of leader. I organise workshops and liaise with people giving direction and support when required. At work in my normal team I tend to be the creative thinker. People come to me for ideas as I am often able to identify better ways of working, but I am not involved in the management of the team.

How well do you take direction from others?

You may be the type of person who seeks reassurance from having the direction and support of others, or find it rather difficult, as you are generally the one who likes to be in charge. You need to:

- Be aware of the roles and responsibilities within the job that you have applied for.
- Appreciate there are times when giving direction is very important; for example, in a crisis situation or when someone is inexperienced in a job. Give an example of when this has happened and how you felt about it.

Do:
- State what the situation was.
- How you dealt with it.
- Explain why you needed direction, did you ask for this or was it provided?
- State what you learnt from it.

Don't:
- Say that you detest being told what to do, when the role clearly indicates you will be managed by others.
- State that you never need the direction of others as you generally get it right first time.

How would you describe your management style?

There are a number of different styles and knowing some of the terminology may help you to describe your approach to managing others. The most important aspect to explain to the interviewer is that you adapt your leadership style to suit the needs of the individuals you are working with. The range of styles and why you would use them are:

- Autocratic: take your own approach, rarely listen to others or ask for contribution, tell others what to do.
- Democratic: encourage input from others, listen to concerns and ideas and build these into decisions where appropriate.
- Directive: useful for inexperienced staff who need to be clear about what is expected of them, also useful in a crisis situation.
- Supportive/coaching: useful for people who have the skills and experience, but need a boost in confidence and motivation.
- Delegative: appropriate when people are capable and motivated to carry out their role.

Example

I am a democratic leader. I encourage my team to contribute, I listen to responses and take on board their ideas and comments and build these into the final decision where necessary. I am also aware of the need to be flexible in my style to suit the needs of the individuals I am working with. For instance, I have a new team member who requires more direction than other members of my staff who are very capable of dealing with issues themselves.

How do you get the best from the people you work with?

They want to know how you recognise that some individuals need a different approach to others. This may not necessarily be in a leadership capacity, but show that you understand how people best learn and take in information. If you are able to adapt your style to suit these people, then inevitably you will get more out of them.

Example

I know my team fairly well having been with them for five years. I recognise that some are more capable than others and some require more detailed instructions from me. For instance, there is one person who takes in information much better if you email it to her, giving lots of detail and facts. Another colleague prefers to have a conversation and to draw a picture of the process and the steps that need to be worked through, to help understand and focus on the task.

Fitting in

How do you ensure you listen to the views of others?

We all think we listen to people, but some of us just don't really. Listening is about hearing what someone says, understanding this and using it or translating it further.

Example

I always encourage people to talk to me and give me their ideas – I don't know everything. I ask a lot of questions and in order to fulfil my role I need to listen and understand what they are saying. I also repeat information back to ensure that I have recorded it correctly.

Have you ever had a disagreement with your manager?

A simple yes or no is not going to suffice, however, that is, of course, the obvious reply. If answering yes, then you need to be prepared to give an example of when this has happened. If answering no, then indicate why you think this may be.

Do:

- Use an example that doesn't paint either yourself or your manager in too bad a light.
- Explain the situation fully and consider addressing the following questions:
  - What was the situation?
  - How did this come about?
  - What did you do, how did you react?
  - What did they do, how did they react?
  - How was this resolved, or was it resolved?
  - What did you do to contribute to the resolution of this disagreement?

Example

We were undertaking a very complex project involving the majority of team members. I realised from an email my manager had sent out that one of the key members of the team was not included. I raised this with my manager presuming my colleague had been missed out by accident. My manager reacted very angrily, stating that the individual did not need to be included. In response to this I asked to see my manager in private to talk about it in more detail as I was leading this project and, in my view, I needed the skills and knowledge of this particular person. I explained this to my manager who was then open with me, stating that the individual had handed in her notice and hence the omission. This was the second resignation my manager had received in the past week and hence the reaction. We talked it through and agreed the individual would be included until she left or a replacement could be found. By addressing the situation straight away and exploring the details we were able to reach an agreement.

> Do not complain or criticise your current or previous companies, boss or colleagues and use them as your reason for looking for a new job. It is best to be positive and complimentary about your current company and boss and focus on the positive things you have gained from working with them. Even if you did work for a dragon, put a positive spin on the situation and don't let the interviewer know.
>
> SUE BARRATT, COUNTRY MANAGER UK, MECCANO TOYS (UK) LTD

Have you ever had a disagreement with a team member?

If you haven't ever had one, then explain why you think that is. Your reasons might include:

- The teams you have worked in have been effective and people have got on well together.
- You have good people skills and will seek to resolve any potential issue before it gets to that point.
- You encourage team members to challenge one another and you, and to discuss issues in an open manner without turning them into a disagreement.

If you have had a disagreement with a team member, try to emphasise the positives from that situation, these could include describing:

- How you handled the situation.
- Identifying what you learnt.
- How the disagreement was resolved.
- How the disagreement could have been avoided in the first place.
- Any benefits for the two of you, or the business, that came out of the disagreement.

Example

I had a disagreement once with a team member about how we should rota the shifts when a new member of staff joined. He had a go at me about the suggestion I had come up with saying that it wasn't fair that he had more late shifts than this new member of staff. In hindsight I should have explained to him that to begin with I couldn't put the new person on a shift with little support so had put the more experienced staff on the late shift. Once I had worked out what the problem was, I took my colleague to one side and explained why I had done it. After that everything was OK.

What frustrates you at work?

You can easily use this question to demonstrate positive qualities about yourself, rather than just describing the petty things that annoy you. Individuals are often frustrated when things don't work smoothly, if work isn't accurate or if people are late or not polite to customers – this actually says they have very high standards of work. Think about the things that frustrate you and see what positive messages these give about you.

Do:
- Indicate why things frustrate you.
- Describe what you have done to improve the situation.
- Describe in a positive way how your frustration shows.

Don't:
- Simply state what aspects about other people or the organisation irritate you.
- Describe any negative behaviour that you demonstrate when feeling frustrated by these things.

Example

I feel quite frustrated at work when, through bad planning, we don't get all our work completed on a daily basis. I like to come in and have a clear desk as I find I am much more productive in this way rather than worrying about how we are ever going to catch up. I have talked to my colleagues about this and as a result we are prioritising work better on a daily basis and being more organised in what we do.

Give an example of when you have admitted to others that you were wrong. Don't see this question as asking you to describe a weakness. Admitting to other that you are wrong is seen as a sign of the ability to reflect on your behaviour and actions and identify improvements, as well as a sign of personal strength. Describe in your answer:

- What the situation was.
- How you realised you were wrong.
- Why you felt it was important to admit this.
- How and who you told you were wrong.
- How you put it right.
- What you learnt from the situation.

Avoid choosing something:
- Very minor.
- With catastrophic consequences – it will be difficult to look good after that.

Example

I once made a decision about how to deal with a customer complaint that wasn't very good. I decided that to get the customer back on board we should give her a £5 credit to her account. Another member of the team said he thought all it needed was an apology and for someone to personally deliver the delayed items of clothing and that person would be fine about it. I didn't really listen to him at the time, but when the customer was still angry with us when she called in to collect the goods, I realised that my colleague was right. I apologised to the customer and my colleague and said I had learnt an important lesson that day about the power of the personal touch over money.

Describe a situation when you have had to demonstrate support for something you didn't entirely agree with.

Whether you are a manager or member of staff sometimes you are placed in this situation and because you are a representative of the organisation it is important to show your support. In your answer include:

- What you were asked to support.
- What you didn't agree with.
- How you dealt with this dilemma.
- How you demonstrated your support.

Example

The organisation I work for was taken over last year by a much larger company. I thought it was really sad – they were so different to how we had always been with our customers, less interested in them as people and more interested in how they could make money from them. I did, however, decide to stick it out and took a job with the new company. To be successful it was important for me to be as positive as before with my customers and colleagues. I found that by doing this and getting to know more about the new owners I was able to see some benefits in their approach.

Give an example of a time when you have disregarded rules at work in order to achieve an outcome.

There are some rules that absolutely have to be followed; otherwise you may be breaking the law or not complying with regulations, and others that on occasions can be viewed more flexibly. The interviewer wants to assess whether or not you understand the difference and if you can justify the actions that you took. Include in your answer any of the points suggested overleaf.

Fitting in

- What the rule was and why you believed it was alright not to adhere to it.
- What you did.
- What the benefits were of doing this – for you and the organisation.
- Anything you would do differently faced with the same situation again.

Example

We had a policy at work that if you were making a payment to a customer in recognition of an error we had made or complaint they had raised, that this always had to be signed off by the area manager. The amounts varied a lot and I think the company thought that this rule would keep control of money being used in this way. We had an occasion when a customer had not received the agreed payment and was creating a scene in the branch – none of the area managers were available as they were away on a conference and it seemed a silly thing to be bothering a director with. I knew the amount that had been discussed so I went ahead and made the transfer there and then – I decided to take any repercussions that might come as a result, but actually it was all fine and I was praised for using my initiative.

How do you feel about working within set guidelines?

Some people need set guidelines to work within and others prefer a less structured approach. The interviewer wants to understand which group you fall into and how you deal with any frustrations that you may encounter because of this. Include in your answer:

- An indication of how you feel about set guidelines.
- What you think the benefits of this and a less structured approach are.
- How you deal with any frustrations that you may have about working in this way.

Don't:
- Demonstrate a negative attitude to set guidelines.
- Indicate that you are useless at this and prefer to work in your own way.

Example

Although I am not always in favour of too many rules and regulations in life I do think it can be helpful at work to have some set guidelines to work to. The benefits of this are that it ensures consistency between my work and that of my colleagues as well as making sure we do all the things that are necessary.

Describe a situation when you have received unfair criticism from others.

It's something that happens and the interviewer wants to know how you react to it when it does. Do you 'go off the deep end' and get upset and angry, do you remain calm and try to find a diplomatic way of pointing out to those concerned that they were wrong, or do you just ignore it? Include in your answer any of the following points:

- What the situation was.
- Why you think you were criticised.
- What was unfair about the criticism.
- What you did to deal with the situation.
- What you learnt from this experience.

Example

There was a situation a few months ago when one of the team leaders had a go at me for not properly completing paperwork on a case file. I felt a bit aggrieved about this as I hadn't realised that I had done anything wrong. After thinking about it for a few days I had a chat with my own line manager and we identified that I needed some further training on this area. Since then I have been able to complete the work to the standard required.

Fitting in

Practicalities

Pay, mobility and other 'housekeeping' issues that the interviewer may be interested in are all covered in this section.

....

What salary are you expecting?

In most cases the salary for the position will have been advertised and therefore you need to be realistic with your response. You could consider:

- The post is advertised at £xk – that is what I am expecting.
- I am currently earning £xk and would be looking for an increase as this role has more responsibility.
- I am currently earning £xk but realise the post is advertised at £xk – so somewhere within this region.

There is no point stating you are looking for £5k more than the post is being advertised at, unless you have already had a conversation with someone within the organisation explaining your situation and they have indicated that this is possible. The interviewer may realise you have experience beyond the position you have applied for and has another post available (now or in the future) that you could be considered for.

Don't:
- Inflate your salary expectation so much that you are out of the running.
- Be unrealistic about your prospective earnings.

What is your present salary?

Again, you should be honest, as you will need to provide your new employer with your P45 detailing your previous earnings, so lying about your salary is out of the question. You may be in a situation of redundancy or have been in a position of temporary employment that does not reflect your potential earnings realistically. If this is the case, then state what you are currently/ previously earning and give a clear indication of what you are expecting – refer to the previous question for suggestions on how to handle this. You will not do yourself any favours by exaggerating your own status and current salary to get additions in your pay packet.

Will you take this job if it is you offered to you?

This is not necessarily a simple yes or no answer. You may want to consider the opportunity further, or weigh it up against other jobs, so don't be pushed into making a decision there and then – they haven't even offered it to you yet. In your answer:

- Indicate that you feel positive about the role and would like to have an offer from them, but would obviously want to think about this – it's a big decision.

You could also consider saying:

- 'Yes I would, without doubt' – without sounding too desperate.
- 'I would give it serious consideration.'
- 'I would like to understand more about the specific role before committing. Is there a way I could shadow someone for a day?'

Avoid saying:
- 'Not on your life' – you never know who you might know who works there or you may want a position with them in the future.
- 'Depends on the package you are going to give me.'

How geographically mobile are you?

There is no point stating that you are willing to move location when really you know you are not. The location of the role should have been detailed within the advertisement or the job description and should not be a surprise to you.

If yes:
- Establish if there is a relocation package attached with the role.
- Ask how much support are they likely to give you.
- Find out if they would provide you with temporary accommodation if required and how long would this be for.

If no:
- You need to be honest as when it comes to the crunch you may be left looking like a time waster and when other vacancies arise within the organisation they may steer clear of your application.

Fitting in

Have you any criminal convictions – spent or unspent?

An employer is permitted to ask if you have any criminal convictions – if you have any that are unspent, you are obliged to declare these. If the conviction is spent or you were given a final warning, reprimand or caution, you do not have to declare those.

Do you require a work permit?

An employer is also entitled to ask this question – your answer need only be a simple 'yes' or 'no'. If the answer is no, it may exclude you from further consideration as the employer may not be able to secure a work permit for the type of vacancy they are seeking to fill. It is important that you are honest about this matter.

How have you made yourself available for this interview while still holding down a job?

Easily explained, but so many people fall into the trap of trusting the interviewer or the receptionist even by saying, 'I phoned in sick. 'You have to question what that says about you and your integrity, would you do the same to them?

A simple 'I took a day's leave' will suffice without having to go into detail as to what illness you have faked, or 'I managed to re-jig my diary between appointments so I could see you.'

Some strange questions

In some interviews you may be asked some of the questions shown below. While they are not quite what you might expect to be asked, they are sometimes used to break the ice or as an indication of how quick thinking you are.

....

If you were a piece of fruit, what would you be?
If you were an animal, what would you be?
If you were a piece of furniture, what would you be?
If you were a nursery rhyme, what would you be?
If you were a cartoon character, what would it be?

In answering these questions:

Do:
● Give an upbeat, fun answer.
● Try to link your answer to some skills or qualities that are relevant to the role you have applied for; for instance, a cat because they are quick witted and independent.
● Be prepared to explain why you would like to be that particular thing.

Don't:
● Say you can't think of anything.
● Just say something such as 'a strawberry', because you like the taste, rather than relating it back to yourself.

Example
If I were a piece of furniture, I would be a bookcase because they contain interesting and entertaining information, are visited by lots of people in the house and even visitors glance at them and comment on their contents.

Sell this desk to me!

The interviewer is interested in your sales approach and how creative and confident you are thinking on your feet. This question could be directed at any article within an office and could be a pen, paperclip or filing cabinet. Although a little off-putting, natural sales people will shine through with this question. You need to consider the suggestions overleaf.

Fitting in

- Giving the factual, descriptive details.
- Speaking enthusiastically and with confidence.
- Smiling!
- Highlighting all of the benefits and avoiding the downsides.
- Keeping it very brief and to the point.
- Allowing your sense of humour to shine through – but keep it appropriate.

Example

There are huge benefits to this desk, it is easily moveable, neutral in colour, provides a good surface space for those people who enjoy hanging on to their paperwork and adheres to all health and safety requirements.

What is your party piece?

This question would be more likely to be asked in an interview where the interviewers are looking for an extraverted person who can grab attention, react quickly, think on their feet and be innovative and fun – sales roles in particular. In your answer:

Do:
- Describe briefly something you can do that perhaps other people can't.
- Indicate a situation when this has been useful.

Don't:
- Describe how much you can drink or a party piece that may cause offence or embarrassment to the interviewer.

Example

My party piece is that I can say the alphabet backwards. I am not sure as to how useful this is, but it amuses others over the dinner table.

8 Changing direction

☑ Understanding your life decision
☑ Coping with the new career

Understanding your life decision

There are sometimes occasions in our working life when we feel we may be in the wrong job or career. Many people take steps to change this and make the brave decision to do something new. This may require them being prepared to retrain, take a cut in salary or take a more junior role.

This section discusses the types of questions that an employer may ask you if you are applying for a job in this situation and provides some guidance on how to answer those questions.

....

What has prompted your change in career direction?

It may be for a wide range of reasons, such as redundancy from a declining industry, you are not enjoying aspects of your current career, or that you have realised that you are better suited to a career in another area. Whatever the reason you need to:

● State clearly your reasons for wanting to change career.
● Describe the process you have gone through to make this decision.
● Remain positive, you may hate your current job, but try to indicate you are unhappy with it in a fairly neutral tone.
● Focus your answer on why you are keen to move into their industry or function.

Example
I am looking to move out of the manufacturing industry, as this is, unfortunately, a contracting area and will, in the long term, limit my career opportunities. I have enjoyed my time in manufacturing but have thought about the skills I have and the other industries I might be suitable for and the design industry seems to be a good match. Not only has it been a growing area over the last few years, it appears also to be a challenging industry to work in.

What are you looking for in a change of career direction?

The interviewer wants to assess how much you have thought this move through and whether you are clear about what your longer-term aims are. You need to:

● Describe what your short- and long-term aims for your career are – even if this is as simple as having a job that you find rewarding.
● Identify clearly how you think the job you have applied for might fulfil these aims.

- Indicate what is really important to you in a job and how this new career would satisfy that.

Example

I am looking to move out of office work into a more customer-focused career as I miss having contact with people in a service environment on a day-to-day basis. I am looking for a more challenging work environment. I have thought about what I am good at and discussed this with colleagues and they all say that it is my interpersonal skills and ability to build relationships that most stands out about me.

> **A good candidate will convince you that they are genuinely interested in the job and the company.**
>
> PHIL MARSLAND,
> HR MANAGER, PORTAKABIN

What career options have you considered?

This question allows you to do two things – indicate the research you have done to reach your decision and your reasons for choosing the industry/job that you are being interviewed for.

Do:

- Describe the research you have done into various jobs/industries.
- State what is important to you in a career/job.
- Indicate briefly the qualities that make you a good candidate.

Don't:

- Indicate that you have looked at loads of options and still can't really decide.
- Say that you are a serial career mover who can never settle.

Example

I have looked at a few new career options including IT and finance, but having done a short general management course feel that marketing is more suited to me. I am attracted by the diverse nature of roles in this area and feel I have the outgoing personality and ability to deal with challenges that would suit me to this kind of work.

What transferable skills do you have?

The interviewer is looking for you to put forward a persuasive argument about the skills and qualities that you have developed in your career to date that would be relevant to the vacancy they are filling.

Do:

- Relate your skills and qualities directly to the ones they are looking for.
- Be honest and realistic about what you will bring to the role.

Changing direction

- Think outside the box – not just about what you have learnt at work.
- Talk about job specific skills and personal qualities, they are both important to employers.

Don't:
- Refer to skills and qualities that are not relevant to the role, even if they are one of your strengths.
- Stretch the truth. For example, managing a household budget does not make you an expert on financial management.

Example
I have developed team leadership skills in my role as a volunteer with a local Nature Conservation Trust. I lead and motivate a team of volunteers to learn and complete tasks, often in quite challenging weather conditions. I am conscious of the fact they don't have to be there and take the time to get to know them and understand what they would like to gain from the experience.

Why didn't you make this change in career sooner?

A difficult question to answer, but one where it is important to be honest without necessarily revealing your complete life history. There is no need to list the many things that have got in the way of you changing career, such as financial commitments, family commitments, or lack of nerve. Include in your answer:

- An indication of whether this move is something you have wanted for a long time or is a recent decision.
- The reasons why now is a good time for you to make this change – both personally and professionally.
- A brief overview of any factors that have constrained you in the past, but are no longer an issue.

Example
I have always wanted to work in the social care sector but understood that I would need to undergo some training and even study for a qualification to do this. I now no longer have the family commitments I used to have and will have the time to focus on developing new skills and the opportunity to do my studying.

REMEMBER!

Avoid blaming others for not having made a move sooner – demonstrate that you take responsibility for your own career and its development.

What skills/knowledge do you think you will have to learn to take up a new career?

You can choose to answer this specifically for the role you are applying for or comment more generally on skills and knowledge that you think you should develop to move on to another career, such as learning about financial services products or developing better IT skills. Include in your answer:

- What skills and knowledge you think you should develop.
- Why these are important for this job or to help you move career.
- Some indication of how you could develop these skills.
- Any steps you have already taken to develop any of these skills.

Example

To take up a career in financial services I think I need to develop a greater knowledge of the range of products that are sold to customers and I could also do with improving my IT skills in the areas of Word and Excel. I have already booked on an evening course to improve these IT skills and would read up on all the various kinds of products using company literature, the internet and attend any relevant courses.

How will you cope with a complete change in working environment after so many years in your current role/career?

In answering this question you need to describe:

- The positive aspects of a new work environment – the things you are looking forward to.
- The challenges you think you may face.
- How you would tackle those challenges.

Example

I think the biggest difference for me in changing career will be to get used to a more modern management style that many companies have, where people are involved in making decisions and work in open-plan offices. Although this may be strange for me at first it is something that I am really looking forward to. What I think I would do is ask immediate colleagues to guide me and tell me how I am doing in the early weeks.

REMEMBER!

Remain upbeat and positive in giving your answer – yes, it may be a real challenge to change career at this stage in your life, but emphasise the positive aspects as much as possible while being realistic.

Changing direction

Coping with the new career

For an employer to take a risk and offer you a role in a different industry or function, they are going to need convincing that you have thought this move through, that you have the right skills for their vacancy and the ability to learn new skills, knowledge and ways of working. The questions around this whole area are likely to be quite searching and extensive, so to make sure you have the best chance of getting the job, do lots of preparation before the interview.

How does your past experience in a different industry qualify you for this role?

As well as assessing transferable skills, the interviewer, in this question, wants to assess whether or not you can see the similarities between different industries. For example, most industries have customers of some kind. In answering this question identify:

- Parallels between the industry you work in now and the one you wish to move into.
- Transferable skills you could use.
- An example of how you could use your previous experience.

Example
I think there are some similarities between the hospitality industry and financial services as customers are key to both and they focus a lot upon results and targets. I have developed skills in working with customers and delivering against targets as well as some team leadership experience that I feel would be invaluable in this role. I feel I would be able to bring a fresh approach to managing staff in a target-led environment because of my previous experience.

What challenges do you feel you will face in this new role?
The interviewer will want to see that you have:

- A realistic understanding of the differences compared to your previous role.
- Identified the challenges you may face.
- Identified how you will deal with those challenges.

Avoid:
Trying to appear confident and well equipped for the role by saying there won't be any real challenges for you – they obviously think there will be otherwise they wouldn't have asked the question.

Example

I think the biggest challenge for me in moving to a role in such a different kind of industry will be understanding the different aspects of that industry, the jargon used and the specific issues it faces. I would overcome this by making sure that I spent time with people across the organisation finding out about what they do, reading the trade journals on a regular basis and discussing my findings with my line manager.

What different challenges do you think you will face working within the public sector after working within the private sector?

Key differences may include a more structured management style, a focus on doing things 'by the book' together with some influences from the political arena, such as doing work for ministers or having to follow the latest government's policy.

Do:
- Describe the key differences.
- State what opportunities or benefits you think these differences may present for you.

Don't:
- Assume there will be no differences – this is likely to concern the interviewer.

Example

Having worked in a commercial organisation I think the biggest difference for me moving to the public sector will be the lack of focus on generating income and the need to think more about ensuring that policies and procedures are followed. I think this would be a good discipline for me to get used to and my ability to deliver results will probably be useful in meeting the objectives that I will be set.

What different challenges do you think you will face working within the private sector after working within the public sector?

Key differences that you may encounter will include a greater focus upon generating income, providing excellent customer service and competing in the marketplace. In addition, many organisations will have a more entrepreneurial approach and will decide what their own priorities are rather than being driven by government policy. In answering this question you should take on board the points overleaf.

- State clearly what you think the differences might be.
- Describe how you would handle those differences.
- Indicate what you find appealing about those differences.

Example

I think the key differences I will find working in the private sector are the need to ensure the company is making money and being less accountable to the taxpayer. I also think I am likely to have greater contact with customers and need to be prepared to be flexible and not always stick to what my job description says.

How quickly do you feel you will be effective in this role?

The answer to this will depend upon how much you think you have to learn. Include the following points:

- A rough guide as to timescales.
- An indication that even in the early days you will be focusing on making whatever contribution you can to the organisation.
- That you have a positive attitude to the learning that you are going to need to do.

Example

I think I should be able to make a general contribution to the team within a few days but it may be some weeks before I can make any significant improvements to what is going on. I would focus my early weeks on understanding the current situation and identifying what could be going better as this appears to be a priority for the team.

Moving up the ladder

☑ Your career to date
☑ Your future career

Your career to date

Some people have a clear career plan and others more of a general view of how they want to progress – even if that is just about having rewarding or interesting work to do. Either way the interviewer will want to understand your career motivations and what steps you have taken to fulfil these.

What are your career ambitions?

The interviewer will be interested to hear whether you have very specific career goals, for example, 'I want to be a manager within five years', or more general aims, such as, 'I want to work in an industry that is fast paced and will provide me with new challenges on an ongoing basis.'

Do:
- Give a brief overview of your specific or general career ambitions.
- State why these ambitions are important to you.

Don't:
- Give a long list of unrealistic ambitions just to try to impress.
- Deny that you have any career ambitions at all.

Example
I would like to have responsibility for a significant part of a business one day, maybe as a manager, and work with a range of different clients and colleagues. I think a job like this would give me the challenge I need and also plenty of variety on a day-to-day basis.

> **REMEMBER!**
>
> *An interviewer is likely to ask searching questions about your motivation for seeking a more senior role and your ability to carry it out successfully – you are a bit of an untested quantity to them and they will need convincing that you are right for their vacancy.*

What is important for you in terms of your career?

This is an open question and one that is designed to find out about you, what motivates you and what your priorities are in terms of your career. Consider including the following in your answer:

- How important personal development opportunities are to you.
- How important career progression is to you.
- What kind of career progression opportunities interest you.
- What kind of challenges you enjoy.
- What kind of balance you like between work and home life.

> A great candidate has full yet concise answers that are relevant, clear and enthusiastic. They will have a fabulous work ethic and well-considered answers that display their values, such as honesty and integrity.
>
> INTERVIEW TEAM, FIRST DIRECT

Example

My career is important to me and I like to feel that I am developing my skills all the time and that there are new challenges that I can take on. I want to be able to make a tangible contribution to an organisation and progress within it as well as enjoy my work.

What does success in your career mean to you?

We all define success very differently – how senior our job is, how rewarding we find our work, being appreciated by others. These are just a few examples of how this question might be answered. Include in your answer:

- A brief summary of what success means to you.
- An indication of how successful you feel you have been to date in your career based on this definition.

Example

To me, success in my career is about having a job that I find challenging and rewarding. The kind of work I have been doing recently has been like that – I really enjoy the responsibility of leading a team, developing their skills and feeling that I am recognised for the contribution I make to the organisation.

Aren't you being unrealistic in terms of your career ambitions?

Quite a challenging question and one it is important you respond to positively. Obviously it is best if you can disagree with the interviewer's suggestion, but you need to do this in a polite and reasoned manner – he or she is probably being deliberately provocative to see whether you are really committed to your plans or have just said something to try and impress.

Example

I am a determined person and like to have goals to aim for. I know that my career ambitions are challenging ones, but I believe that as long as I keep focused upon them and put in the work that is required that I can achieve them. I have already made good progress by passing my management diploma and gaining some team leadership experience.

Moving up the ladder

How satisfied are you with the speed at which your career has progressed?

However you feel about your career progression, include the following points in your answer:

- Why you are/aren't satisfied with progress.
- What you would do differently.
- What you have learnt about career progression.

Avoid:
- Simply stating you are very satisfied with the progress of your career.
- Being too negative about the state of your career.
- Blaming other people for why you are stuck where you are.

Example

Yes, generally, I am happy with the speed that my career has progressed. I think so far I have managed to develop my skills in a number of areas by staying in roles for at least a couple of years. In future I will continue to keep developing my experience to reach my overall career goal.

If you started your career again, what would you do differently?

You can choose to answer this question by describing a dream job you would like to have had but indicate why that wasn't realistic – such as being a fighter pilot, but you have poor eyesight – or identify something in your actual career that you think could have been better or different.

Avoid:
- Listing too many regrets.
- Blaming other people for what has happened to you.

Example

On the whole I have been happy with my career and how it has worked out. I think the only thing I might change is that I could have made the move from retail to financial services sooner. I don't regret the time I spent working in retail as I learnt a lot of useful things but I could probably have moved on a year or two sooner.

What have been the highlights of your career to date?

This question allows you to talk about what you have achieved that you are proud of, for example, 'I was appointed a manager at the age of 25', or a significant piece of work that you feel went particularly well, such as, 'leading a team of ten people over a six-month period to deliver the x project on time and within budget.'

Example

I am particularly proud of the contribution I have made over the last two years to the changes the company has gone through. I have been instrumental in leading a number of teams through this change and the work has been recognised in my recent promotion to regional manager.

What other areas in an organisation would you like to gain experience of working in?

An open question that you can choose to answer in two ways: 'I really love the area I work in but recognise it might be useful to have a better understanding of what other people do', or, 'I would like to gain experience of working in another area as I think it would be something I would be good at and be interested in.' Include in your answer:

● What other area you would like to work in.
● Why you would like to work in that area.

Example

I would like to work in the branch network for a while – I feel it would give me a better understanding of the challenges they face and, therefore, I would be more able to provide them with the support they need.

> **TOP TIP**
>
> If you are more interested in staying in the area you currently work in and developing your career there, then say so, otherwise you might find them offering you a transfer one day that you really don't want to take.

Your CV indicates you have been with your current employer for a long time with little advancement. Why is that?

Explain clearly the reasons for this. Was it that you have been very happy there and had lots of new challenges, even though you weren't promoted or maybe there were few opportunities for promotion as people tended to stay with the company until they retired?

Example

Although I have only had two job titles at my current employer the work over the years has always been varied and challenging – lots of things have changed in the business and I have been involved in making these happen. As it is only a small company I feel that I would now like to move onto a larger business and develop my career further.

> **REMEMBER!**
>
> *Always present a positive image of yourself and avoid blaming other people for your lack of advancement or appearing negative about your career with that company.*

Your future career

This section looks at the questions you may be asked about your ambitions for the future, particularly if you are seeking a promotion or more senior job. These will apply whether you are applying for a role with a new organisation or your current employer.

··

What targets have you set yourself in terms of your career?

Your answer to this question should be focused upon specific timescales, qualifications or positions that you are aiming to achieve in your career. Include in your answer:

● What the specific targets are that you have set yourself.
● Why you have set yourself these targets.
● How you intend to achieve the targets.
● How well you are progressing against the targets.

Example

I aim to be a qualified accountant in the next five years. I have already enrolled at college part time and am fitting in doing the required qualifications alongside my current job. Although my employer is very supportive there is limited opportunity with them to gain experience in the finance area as they are a very small company, so I am looking for a junior finance role in a larger organisation like yours.

What sacrifices are you willing to make in order to succeed?

The interviewer wants to assess how flexible you are prepared to be, how driven you are to achieve and where your priorities with other aspects of your life come compared to work.

Do:
● State clearly in what ways you are prepared to be flexible to meet work demands.
● How important your career is to you.
● Any particular sacrifices you are prepared to make to succeed at work.

Don't:
● Say something you would not be prepared to do.
● Feel pressured into saying that work is everything to you – most employers prefer to have staff with a balanced work/personal life approach.

Example

I recognise that to progress it is important to work hard and put the hours in. I am happy to be flexible and am definitely not a nine-to-five kind of person and will often take work home to finish off overnight. However, I do believe I perform better at work if I am rested and have had time doing other things. I am an active sports person and enjoy spending time running and sailing.

How has your current role prepared you for taking on greater responsibilities?

Indicate clearly:

- The experience you have had in your current role that is relevant.
- The skills you have developed that are relevant.
- How you feel about taking on greater responsibilities.

Example

I have often had to stand in for my senior colleague when she is away on holiday and this has taught me different aspects of our work and given me more experience of liaising with colleagues across the organisation. I have also had to take charge of scheduling work for the team. I feel very positive about taking on responsibilities like these on a more permanent basis.

What skills/knowledge would you like to develop in this new position?

Indicate clearly in your answer:

- The skills and knowledge you know you will need to learn to carry out the role.
- The skills and knowledge that you believe will help you continue to develop your career, but are also relevant to the organisation you are applying to.

Answering this question well will also indicate to the interviewer that you have a good understanding of the job and your own development needs.

Example

I would like to learn more about using and analysing the performance data that is produced for the department as well as spending time with other team leaders seeing how they go about running their teams.

How will you approach this new role?

Do you have a plan of action if you are successful in getting the job? What would you do in the first few weeks/months? These are the kinds of things the interviewer wants to hear about as well as any longer-term thoughts on how you would approach the job. In your answer include:

- Actions you would take initially.
- Actions you would take in the longer term.

Example

I would spend the first few days learning more about my responsibilities and the people I was going to be working with. I would also like to introduce myself to colleagues in other departments and go out to meet our customers. In the longer term I would be looking for things that could be improved and how business could be increased.

What do you see as the main priorities in this new role?

The interviewers will want to know whether or not you have developed a good understanding of the role from your research and what they have told you, particularly as the new role is more senior than your previous one. Include in your answer:

- Clear priorities – two or three will be fine.
- A brief indication of how you would tackle these priorities.

Example

I think the immediate priorities in this role are to make sure the team are working well together and that production levels are increased. I would tackle these by getting the team together on a regular basis to build team spirit and by looking at how we could improve the current production process to increase productivity.

Why do you want to move into a management role?

Making the move into a team leader or management role can be a big step up from being one of the team. The interviewer will want to assess your motivation for doing this – is it for the money, the kudos, the power, the sense of responsibility, the ability to influence what is going on in the organisation, or the opportunity to develop others?

Do:

- Give clear reasons for wanting to be a manager.
- Indicate that you have an understanding of the additional tasks and responsibilities this would bring.

Don't:

- Indicate that you see it as a reward for all the years of hard work you have done.
- Indicate you think that at your age you should be a manager.

Example

I would like to move into a management role as I think I have now developed the people management and business skills to do this successfully. I would also relish the opportunity to take on the greater responsibility that comes with such a role and become involved in influencing the direction of the organisation.

What experience do you have of leading or managing others?

This needn't be limited to work-based experience – you may have had to lead a team of volunteers – or to your current role, perhaps you have been asked to lead small project teams or tasks. In your answer describe:

- The occasions you have led teams.
- A brief overview of the team, its size and the task they had to complete.
- The skills you feel you developed.

Example

I was responsible for leading a small team last year for a couple of months when we organised the office move for the department. There were four of us in the team and I developed some really valuable experience in getting the team to decide what needed to be done, how best to use our various skills and motivating them when things got difficult.

What qualities do you have that would make you a good manager?

In answering this question limit yourself to three or four qualities. This will have greater impact than a long list and allow you some time to also indicate briefly how you have used the qualities to good effect. Focus on qualities that:

- Demonstrate that you can manage, lead and motivate people.
- Demonstrate that you can deliver business results.

Moving up the ladder

Example

I believe that I have good interpersonal skills and this would allow me to build strong working relationships with my team, listen to their ideas and concerns and praise and encourage them. I have a good understanding of the business and how targets can be met and would work to focus the team on delivering these.

What have you learnt from previous managers – positive and negative – about leading a team?

Limit yourself to a couple of positive and negative learning points about people you have worked for and their management style. Avoid making your negative comments from a personal point of view, but more generally about how people found it working for that person. In preparing your answer think about all aspects of a managers role, including:

- Managing and motivating people.
- Developing the team.
- Working with other managers.
- Creating plans and measuring performance.

Example

I learnt from one of my early managers the importance of consulting with staff, involving them in decision making and adapting your style of management to suit their needs. Newer, inexperienced staff need more support and guidance than those that are confident in their abilities. From a more negative experience I also learnt that staff don't like it if managers continually criticise people and make fun of those individuals who are still learning the job, and inevitably make some mistakes.

10 Competency based questions

☑ What are competencies?
☑ 20 competencies to prepare answers for

What are competencies?

An increasingly popular approach to assessing candidates is to use a competency or structured interview approach. This chapter explains what competencies are, the theory behind the approach and how to prepare for these interviews. In addition, there is guidance on 20 competencies, what the interviewer will be looking for and the kinds of questions you may be asked.

Competency based interviews and why they are used

Competencies are a way of illustrating the skills, abilities and characteristics required for successful performance in a role that describes the behaviour an individual will display.

We all know there is more than one way to do a job – for example, one person's approach may achieve good sales results but upset customers, while a colleague may rely more on building longer-term relationships with a customer and achieve the same sales results without the hard sell approach.

Competencies allow organisations to make it clear to staff what kinds of behaviours they value and would like to see them displaying, such as team working and communication, and assess new staff against the same criteria. Competencies often form the basis of all recruitment, training and appraisal of staff.

Essentially a company is saying they are as concerned with how you carry out your work as well as the results you achieve.

Competency based interviews work on the principle that the most accurate way of predicting future behaviour and performance is to understand how you have worked in the past. Interviewers assess this by asking individuals to provide real examples of situations they have been in.

> **REMEMBER!**
>
> *There are no right and wrong answers to questions asked at competency based interviews. The interviewer wants to understand your approach to situations you have encountered.*

When asked to give examples of competencies in interviews write them down immediately after the interview to avoid repeating them at a later interview.

RESOURCING TEAM, VODAFONE UK

This kind of interview will no doubt feel very different to a traditional CV-based interview and may give you little opportunity to talk more generally about yourself.

During the interview you will be asked to choose and describe situations that demonstrate the competencies being assessed.

How do I prepare for a competency based interview?

There are number of things you can do in preparation for a competency based interview.

Familiarise yourself with the competencies required for the role. There will be clues to what these are in the job advertisement or job description, and if you are really lucky, you will be told what these are when you are invited for the interview.

Think back over the last couple of years and identify situations at, or outside, work where you have demonstrated these competencies. It is best, but not essential, to keep to recent situations as those over two years may be difficult to recall in sufficient detail. In preparing your examples, think about each situation in the order of the following approach (STAR):

> ### TOP TIPS
>
> - Many interviewers are happy for you to take notes into the interview, so check to see if this is the case for your interview.
> - If you do take notes into an interview, keep them in bullet point format.
> - Make sure you answer the question they have asked you rather than insisting on using an example that doesn't really address the issue just because you have pre-prepared it.

Situation: What was the situation?
Task: What was the specific task you had to achieve?
Action: What specific actions did you take?
Result: What was the outcome of your actions?

Although you won't know the exact questions you are going to be asked, you will find answering the questions posed much easier if you have some situations already in your mind that you have thought about.

Is it OK to use examples from outside work?

Yes, this is fine as long as you are demonstrating the behaviours and qualities the interviewer is looking for. Voluntary work, sports activities and other hobbies can provide very good evidence, but be realistic – if they are asking about how you deliver results, then a work-based example is probably going to be best.

Team working

In questions about team working the interviewer wants to understand whether you work well with colleagues, willingly support others in their work and consider the good of the team before yourself. In other words, do you make a full contribution to the team effort?

Describe a situation when you have worked as part of a team to achieve a task/objective.

This question allows you to choose an example from a wide range of situations – everyday work, special projects or a crisis situation. The interviewer is interested in:

- What was the task you had to achieve.
- What your contribution to the team effort was.
- What actions you took as a group that showed you were co-operating with each other as well as supporting one another.
- What result was achieved.
- What you think the benefits were of working as a team in this situation.

> **REMEMBER!**
>
> *Just give a brief overview of the situation you were in and the task you had to achieve allowing maximum focus and time for talking about how you worked with other people and describing what your contribution was.*

Example

When I was working in the customer contact team for the council we had a period of a few days when we were very short staffed because of holidays and attendance on training courses. We were concerned that we weren't going to be able to keep up with all the phone calls at busy periods and would miss the target of answering calls within 30 seconds.

I suggested that we discuss what we could do as a team and we came up with the idea of dealing with the easy queries that came in straight away and if it was something more complicated taking down the caller's details and question and asking if it was OK if we called back later on in the day.

I discussed this suggestion with our manager and she said it was a good way forward so we gave it a try. It worked really well – especially when we also spotted that we could get one of the more experienced team members working on the queries while others focused on keeping the phones answered.

By doing this we were still able to meet our targets, kept the customers happy and got through all the work that needed doing. It was also a good way of using the skills of the different team members to achieve the task.

Give an example of when you have proactively sought to involve others in a task because of their skills or knowledge.

Focus on the specifics of this question – pick an example that isn't just about team working, but an occasion when you involved others because you needed their help and expertise or because you thought it would be a good opportunity to get them involved in a task. The interviewer will be interested in hearing about:

- How you identified what support or skills you needed.
- How you identified appropriate people to involve.
- What you did to motivate them to assist you.
- What you did to help them understand what help was needed.
- What the outcome was of working in this way.
- What you think the benefits and drawbacks were of taking this approach to your task.

Describe an occasion when you have actively provided support to colleagues in order to achieve team objectives.

The interviewer wants to assess whether you are able to identify when colleagues need support and if you are the kind of person who will go out of your way to give this support. You should include the following points in your answer:

- How you identified they needed support.
- What support they needed – was it practical help, some advice, development or encouragement.
- How you worked with them rather than just taking work off them.
- How you ensured you still did your own work as well as helping your colleague/s.
- What the benefits of doing this were for you, the other person and the team.

REMEMBER!

Your evidence will be stronger if you describe an occasion when you took the initiative in offering help to your colleagues, not one where you were asked to assist someone.

Give an example of how you have encouraged and fostered a team working culture.

This question allows you to describe either an initiative taken with a specific team or contributions you have made at a wider, organisational level to ensure team working is valued. The interviewer will want to assess the points overleaf.

Competency based questions

- What you understand team working to be.
- Whether you are proactive in encouraging others to work as a team.
- What practical actions you took to encourage team working.
- What you did to act as a role model to others, demonstrating the team working behaviours.
- Why you felt it was important to encourage team working.

REMEMBER!

Emphasise the positive effects on the organisation and its performance of having a team working culture – it's not just a nice thing to do.

Describe an occasion when you have had to resolve conflict in a team you were working in.

The interviewer is interested in hearing:

- A brief summary of the conflict.
- What actions you took to resolve this conflict.
- How you were sensitive to the individuals concerned.
- How you took action rather than hoping it would go away.
- How you remained focused on resolving the issue for the benefit of the team.
- What the result of your interventions was, immediately and in the longer term.

REMEMBER!

Choose an example that had a positive outcome, you will look better. This may sound obvious, but you would be surprised how many people don't do this.

TOP TIPS

Avoid talking about what 'we' did too much and remember to use the phrase 'I'. Although this is a team working competency they are interviewing you, not the rest of the team, and want to know what your contribution was.

Communicating and influencing

In asking questions about communication and influencing the interviewer wants to assess whether you can communicate effectively with others, adapt your style or method of communication to suit the audience and if you appreciate the importance of influencing someone by adapting your message to fit with what the listener is interested in.

....

Give an example of a time when you have had to communicate complex information to a colleague or customer.

Choose a situation when it was complex information rather than something straightforward that you had to communicate – maybe a new product, service or process. The interviewer will want to assess:

- Did you translate the information into appropriate, jargon-free language for the listener.
- How you established what their current level of knowledge was.
- How you decided the best way to communicate the information.
- Did you use a range of methods to communicate the information; for example, the spoken word, diagram or visual guide?
- How you checked they had understood what you had communicated.

> **Try to strike a balance between friendly/warm and professional, and talk positively about previous employers.**
>
> INTERVIEW TEAM, FIRST DIRECT

Describe an occasion when you have used various methods of communication to get a message across to different individuals.

This question allows you to show that you understand that people take in information differently – listening, reading, pictures and diagrams, or practical application – and to be effective in communication it is good to use more than one method. A training course you have run or briefing session for colleagues would make a good example. The interviewer will want to hear about:

- Your understanding of the different ways people process information.
- The methods of communication you used.
- Why you used these particular methods.
- How you checked the individuals had understood.
- Anything you learnt from this situation.

Give an example of how you have worked to ensure that critical information is communicated effectively to others.

This question allows you to describe either an initiative taken with a specific team or contributions you have made at a wider, organisational level, to ensure that critical information is communicated consistently to staff. The interviewer will be interested to hear about:

- What the critical information was.
- What obstacles you had to overcome.
- How you overcame these obstacles.
- How you evaluated the success of what you had done.
- What the outcome was of your actions.

Give an example of a time when you had to communicate a difficult/unpopular message to colleagues.

Interviewers want to assess how you approached a sensitive and challenging situation – did you think about how others would feel or more about protecting yourself from blame? Did you take ownership of the information and represent the company viewpoint while at the same time demonstrating empathy and concern for your colleagues? Include in your answer:

- A description of the information you had to communicate.
- What was sensitive or unpopular about this information.
- How you communicated the information.
- Why you communicated in that way.
- What you did to understand the concerns and viewpoints of your colleagues.
- How you responded to these concerns.
- What you learnt from the situation.

Example

The company was undergoing a restructure and part of this meant that there was going to be substantial job losses, which, in turn, was going to affect my department. I was faced with the difficult task of explaining this to my team. I was obliged to follow the company procedures and guidelines for this, but that didn't mean that I couldn't deliver this in a manner I felt suitable for my specific team members.

I knew it was going to affect some of my staff members badly; it was, after all, their livelihood we were talking about. I made the decision to tell everyone together initially to ensure each person received the same information at the same time. Coupled with this I gave out handouts to individuals as, at times like these, some people struggle to take in such information verbally, they need something to go away and think about.

I answered questions and explained the process fully using diagrams for easier understanding. I encouraged an open door policy and arranged meetings with individual team members who wanted to meet with me. It was important in such emotional situations that people were given one-to-one time.

I ensured I kept people informed of progress at all times. It was a very difficult time but I learnt to keep a healthy distance from individuals so that I could give them the best support and advice possible.

Describe an occasion when you have had to persuade someone to your way of thinking.

The interviewer wants to assess the approach you take to doing this. They will want to see if you appreciate the importance of understanding the audience, and adapting your message to fit with this. For example, if you are persuading a logical, rational person, you concentrate on communicating facts and the reasons behind your idea. The interviewer will be interested in hearing about:

- What you were seeking to persuade someone to agree to.
- How you assessed the interests/motivations of that person.
- How you adapted your argument to suit his or her interests.
- How you communicated with that person.
- What the outcome was.

REMEMBER!

Again, try to choose an example with a positive outcome, it will be so much more powerful than one that didn't go very well.

TOP TIP

Successful communication is all about seeing things from the listener's point of view, so make sure you include this in your answer.

Competency based questions

Customer service

Customer service is a hot topic for most organisations. Even those that are not in the more traditional service industries of retail and hospitality like to see both internal colleagues and external contacts as customers and strive to ensure that their needs are understood and met.

....

Describe an occasion when you went over and above what was expected of you to provide excellent service to a customer.

Provide an example when you really did go beyond what would normally be expected of you to help the customer and not just describe a day-to-day activity. Examples might include delivering an item to a customer's home after work or taking on some extra work or responsibilities to help a colleague or another department. It is important to include some evidence of how you understood what the customer wanted from you rather than assuming that you knew this. Follow-on questions might include:

● What was the situation?
● What actions did you take to provide excellent customer service?
● Why was it important to exceed the customer's expectations?
● What feedback did you receive?
● What did you learn from this situation?

Example
The situation was when I was working for X retailer and it was Christmas Eve. I was the supervisor on the day for the food hall, which, as you can imagine, was extremely busy. A customer arrived and went to the pre-order collection point to pick up her turkey. She handed over the relevant paperwork. It became apparent that her turkey was not there and her order had not been processed correctly when she placed it.

She was distraught and was becoming upset. One of my team made me aware of the situation and I took over and asked the lady to come with me to the customer waiting area. I confirmed all of the details with her, offered her a drink and then made some calls to other stores within the region.

I managed to locate a suitable turkey at another store. I informed the lady of where the turkey was, but she had no means of getting there and said actually why should she, it was our error. I arranged to pick up the turkey myself after work and delivered it to the lady's house.

In addition, we gave her a complimentary bottle of champagne for her patience. I don't think there was anything else I could have done. She was delighted and thanked me very much for what I had done. I learnt that most things can be resolved, you may just need to put yourself out to do it.

Describe an occasion when you have sought and responded to customer feedback to improve service levels.

The interviewer wants to assess whether or not you proactively seek customer feedback and if you can provide evidence of having listened to this and taken action as a result of it. Think of an example when you were able to make improvements that resulted in future customers receiving a better service. For example, the telephone is answered more promptly, delivery times are reduced or staff have a better understanding of what the customer considers to be good service. Include the following points in your answer:

- What the situation was.
- How you sought feedback from the customer.
- What the feedback was.
- What improvements you made as a result of this feedback.
- How you measured the success of these improvements.

Describe an occasion when you have had a challenging customer issue to resolve.

In asking this question employers want to assess whether you understand the importance of the relationships with its customers and the impact these have upon business results and company image. In dealing well with a difficult customer encounter, or even a complaint, it is often possible to make the customer feel more positive about the organisation than if the issue had never arisen. Include in your answer:

- What the issue was you had to resolve.
- How the issue had arisen.
- What you did to manage the issue.
- Why you took this approach to managing the issue.
- What you achieved by managing the issue in this way.
- How you managed the customer throughout this process.
- What feedback you had from the customer.
- How you improved service levels as a result of this issue.

Give an example when you have changed processes to deliver an improved customer experience.

Choose an example when you have recognised an issue or inefficiency with the way you or the team are working that was impacting upon the level of service provided for customers. Examples might include changing lunch breaks so there was better cover over the busy period of the day or putting more staff on a project at the start so that it was delivered more quickly for the client. Consider including the following points in your answer:

- What the issue with customer service was.
- How you identified the issue.
- Who you involved in seeking a solution to the issue.
- What changes you made to ensure service levels improved.
- How you measured the success of these changes.
- What improvements you were able to achieve.

Give an example of a time when you have not been able to resolve a customer issue.

It is not always possible to satisfactorily resolve a customer issue or complaint – sometimes we are limited by company policy or procedure or what the customer wants is unrealistic. What is important is that you tried to seek a solution and have learnt from the situation. The interviewer will want to assess:

> **REMEMBER!**
>
> *If you were limited by company policy, include in your answer how you have fed back the issue to the organisation so that they can consider whether they need to change policy or procedure in that area in order to provide a better service to customers.*

- What the customer issue was.
- How you sought to resolve the issue.
- What aspects you were unable to resolve and why.
- How you managed the relationship with the customer.
- What you learnt from this situation.

Driving for results

Having a strong focus upon driving for results is important to many employers
– if they give you the job, they want to know you will deliver results. When
asking questions about this, interviewers want to be provided with clear examples
of occasions when you have taken action to ensure that results were achieved.

Describe an occasion when you had to take action to ensure that you met challenging targets or objectives at work.

Pick an occasion that was challenging – you were behind target or you were
working in a particularly difficult situation or trying
to resolve a complicated issue. The interviewer
will want to hear about:

- What the situation was and why it was challenging.
- Why you felt it was important to achieve targets or objectives.
- What you did, over and above your usual approach, to make sure you delivered results.
- What results you managed to achieve.
- What you learnt from this situation.

> **REMEMBER!**
>
> *Try to quote results – numbers achieved or what the objective was. Saying, 'I achieved the required 20 per cent increase in sales' is a much stronger answer than 'I increased sales.' It gives the interviewer a clearer idea of what you are really capable of.*

Give an example of a time when you identified significant barriers to success for yourself, or others, and have taken action to overcome these.

The interviewer wants to assess whether or not you are able to identify what
the barriers to achieving results can be and how you have gone about
overcoming these. Barriers might include lack of resource, lack of time or
change in circumstances since the objectives were set. Include in your answer:

- What the barriers to success were.
- How you identified the right way of overcoming these barriers.
- What actions you took to overcome the barriers.
- Who you needed support from.
- How you won the support of these individuals.
- What outcome you achieved.
- How this situation has changed the way you work.

Describe an occasion when you have taken action to develop a performance-based culture in a team/organisation.

This question allows you to describe either an initiative taken with a specific team or contributions you have made at a wider, organisational level to ensure staff focus upon achieving results. The example should illustrate what you have done to change the longer-term behaviour of people, such as regularly reviewing performance, basing pay on results or providing easily seen reminders of how the team is doing on a daily basis, such as by creating charts. To provide strong evidence in answering this question you should consider covering the following:

● What the initial situation was.
● What you wanted to achieve.
● What factors you considered in seeking to change the culture.
● What actions you took to change the culture.
● What results you achieved.

Example

When I took over my new team it became apparent very quickly that they were unaware of their targets and objectives or how they were performing against these. They had been given little direction and support previously so I guess this was no great surprise. I needed to first get them to understand what the targets were and why they were so important. I held a team briefing initially and a brainstorming session to raise awareness and then weekly meetings from there on in.

I was really impressed how quickly everyone got up to speed and for those people that needed more support I held one-to-one coaching sessions and used the skills and abilities of others in the team to help support those less confident members. I used a variety of methods of communication within the meetings, sometimes visual prompts, and sometimes role-play situations, where appropriate.

I also introduced a competitive element to this, but made sure it was a bit of fun and had everyone's support for the idea before doing so. The results soon spoke for themselves and within two months we had hit target and were on schedule for the next month. Coupled with this, each member of the team was well aware of what they were doing in terms of targets and why.

Give me an example of when you have set challenging objectives for yourself/your team.

In asking this question the interviewer will want to assess whether you are the kind of person who will stretch themselves/their team to deliver results for the organisation or if you are more concerned about doing the minimum that is required. They will want to hear about the points described opposite.

- Why you thought it was important to set challenging objectives.
- What objectives you set.
- What actions you took to ensure the objectives were met.
- What results you achieved.

Give an example of when you have delivered results that were over and above what was required of you.

The interviewer wants to assess whether you are the kind of person who will drive themselves to achieve more than is expected and what might make you do that. Include in your answer:

- What the situation was.
- Why you wanted to overachieve.
- What actions you took to overachieve.
- What results you achieved.
- What were the benefits for the organisation/yourself.
- What you learnt from this situation.

Developing yourself

In asking questions about developing yourself interviewers want to assess whether you take responsibility for your own development or leave it to your employer, have any long-term interest in developing skills for your career and recognise the importance of ongoing development in order to be effective in your work.

....

Describe what you do on an ongoing basis to keep yourself up to date within your industry/knowledge area.

Focus on what you do on an ongoing basis to develop your knowledge as the main part of your answer rather than any specific training you have done. Describe how you keep yourself up to date with the industry you work in as well as the particular function that your job relates to. Also indicate clearly why you think it is important to keep up to date with what is going on in your industry – this may be due to the rapid changing nature of the area you work in or in order to develop yourself for the benefit of your ongoing career. The interviewer will want to assess the following:

- What you have identified as important information to keep up to date with.
- How you keep yourself up to date.
- How you fit this around your work/personal life.
- How you have applied this knowledge at work.

Give an example of when you have taken action to develop yourself to meet the needs of your role.

When answering this question pick a situation when you had to develop specific skills or knowledge to carry out your role. For instance, you could refer to learning about a new product or system, developing better IT skills or improving how you communicate with colleagues. Say, too, when you took the initiative to develop these yourself or in your own time rather than being sent on a course by your employer. The interviewer will be interested to hear about:

- What skills/knowledge you wanted to develop.
- Why it was important to develop these.
- What you did to develop yourself.
- How you have used your learning in the workplace.

Example

When I was promoted into a team leader position I realised that although I had the core skills and some brief experience of leading others outside of work, I needed some support and advice on better ways of dealing with people in order to get the best from them.

I did some research into specific team leadership courses that were available and spoke to my manager about these. He agreed and I booked myself in. I really enjoyed the interaction on the course, learning from others and sharing experiences.

I learnt some really useful techniques in terms of motivating others, offering coaching and support and identifying where and how to adapt my style to suit the needs of others. The coaching skills I learnt were put into practice very soon after returning from the course as one of the team members was struggling to achieve her target. We undertook various coaching sessions and within a month she was on target. After two years now within this role I feel I am able to cope with a variety of situations involving staff members.

Describe an occasion when you have sought feedback from colleagues at work and acted upon it to improve your performance.

This question provides you with the opportunity to demonstrate that you are the kind of person who actively seeks feedback on your approach to work from colleagues, staff or your manager and then takes some action to change or improve your performance as a result. The interviewer will want to assess:

- Who you sought feedback from.
- Why you asked for feedback.
- What feedback you were given.
- What you did as a result of this feedback.
- How you have applied this learning over the longer term.

Pick a situation where you actually sought the feedback rather than it being volunteered. Also choose feedback that has been particularly helpful to you in your work since that day.

Describe the actions you have taken to develop yourself for your longer-term career.

Focus your answer on any development you have undertaken that was in support of longer-term career goals rather than to equip you for your current job. Examples might include management or vocational qualifications, gaining experience of working in different industries or situations by volunteering or being seconded to another job or asking someone to mentor you. Interviewers will be interested to hear about the suggestions given overleaf.

- What your long-term career goals were.
- What development you undertook.
- How you managed this alongside your job/personal life.
- What you learnt or developed.
- How you have applied this learning.

Describe a situation that illustrates how you have applied learning in the workplace.

Employers are more impressed by initiatives that people have taken to develop themselves if the learning has actually been applied at work rather than something that seemed interesting to do. Better to talk about the management book you have read than the flower-arranging course you went on. Pick an example where you are able to demonstrate benefits for both you and the organisation in applying the learning. The interviewer will want to hear about:

- What the learning was.
- How you had gained this new skill/knowledge.
- How you applied the learning at work.
- What the benefits were for you and the organisation.

Your answer will be stronger if you can describe learning that set you apart from your colleagues or was something new for the team or department you were working in; such as, learning a piece of software that no one else knew how to use.

TOP TIP

Development isn't just about training courses – it may be books you have read, different work, voluntary experiences or coaching from a colleague.

Developing others

In asking questions about developing others, employers want to assess whether you support the training and development of colleagues and staff and are prepared to put time and effort into this critical activity, or are more focused upon your own development needs.

....

Give an example of an occasion when you have helped train or develop a colleague.

This question allows you to talk about a specific day/time when you trained a colleague on a task or when you helped develop someone's skills over a longer period of time. The interviewer will want to hear about:

- What the training needs of the colleague were.
- How you established what they already knew and where the shortfalls were.
- How you went about training/developing the person.
- How you adapted your style to suit the individual concerned.
- What feedback you had on what you had done.
- What the outcome was of you helping the colleague – emphasise the benefits that arose.

Example

We had a new person start within the team. It has been sometime since we had had someone new so we all needed to recognise how we could help and support him. I was responsible for taking him through his induction training and explaining the main areas of responsibility within the role.

After spending some time with the new person I was able to understand what the training needed to focus upon. I had an experienced team so I allocated specific people to train him in the different areas of work. This was a good opportunity for team members to develop coaching and training skills as well as develop the individual.

The results were really positive. The new team member received a variety of different opinions and training styles and he was able to integrate so much more quickly within the team. Feedback was really positive from the team and the individual. I shared this approach with my colleagues, who have adopted the same process with their new people.

Describe an occasion when you have planned and supported the development of a member of your team.

The interviewer wants to assess if you take a planned or ad hoc approach to developing your team, whether or not you put time aside to support their development personally or send them on a training course, and how effective you have been in developing others. Include in your answer:

- How you assessed what the training or development needs of the individual were.
- What you did to ensure they were committed to developing.
- How you planned the training or development.
- What support you provided personally.
- How you measured progress and the success of the training or development.
- How you monitored progress of the individual.
- What you learnt from this situation.

Describe an occasion when you have taken action to put in place processes to enable the development of others across the organisation.

Focus upon how you have influenced or contributed to the development of staff across the organisation rather than just your own team or immediate colleagues. Examples could include championing a particular training programme, ensuring greater emphasis upon development of staff by managers or putting in place a personal development planning process for staff. Areas to include in your answer are:

- Why you thought it was important to enable the development of others.
- What you wanted to achieve.
- What steps you took.
- How you measured the success of what you had done.
- What the outcome was and how it benefited the organisation and the individuals involved.
- Anything you would have done differently.

Give an example of a time when you should have taken more action to help train/develop a colleague or member of staff.

The interviewer wants to assess whether or not you reflect on your approach to development and can identify an occasion when you could have done more. They will be interested to hear about:

- What development needs the individual had.
- What action you took to support them.
- What was missing from the support you gave them.

- How this became apparent.
- What remedial action you took to put the situation right.
- What you learnt from the situation.
- How you have applied this learning to other situations.

Describe an occasion when you have acted as a coach or mentor to someone.

This question allows you to demonstrate any skills and experience you have in coaching or mentoring someone as opposed to more traditional approaches to development such as training. The interviewer will want to assess your level of understanding of such a role, your ability to allow the individual to direct their own learning and how you have approached challenging them and acting as a 'sounding board'. They will be interested in hearing about:

- How you became involved as a coach or mentor.
- What approach you took to coaching or mentoring the individual.
- Why you took this approach.
- What results you achieved with the individual.
- Anything you learnt from this experience.
- What you found to be the most challenging and rewarding aspects of being a coach or mentor.

TOP TIP

When answering questions on developing others, remember to include how you assessed or understood what the learning needs of the individual or group were rather than assuming that you knew.

Building relationships

Many jobs require the ability to develop positive, ongoing working relationships with customers, colleagues, external partners or stakeholders. In asking questions about this competency, interviewers want to assess whether you have an understanding of how to do this effectively, experience of building relationships with a wide range of people and demonstrate the approach that will generate a long-term business relationship.

···

Describe a relationship you have built with a customer that has been beneficial for the organisation.

This question allows you to describe either a relationship you built with an individual customer or individuals within a larger corporate customer that have resulted in increased business for your organisation. The interviewer will be interested to hear about:

- Who the customer was.
- Why you wanted to develop a good relationship with them.
- What you did to build the relationship.
- What you did to ensure that the relationship continued after the initial meeting/business transaction.
- How was the relationship beneficial to your organisation.
- What you learnt from this situation.

> **REMEMBER!**
>
> *Choose an example where you were successful in securing business benefits from the relationship – it is not just about them thinking that you are a nice person who gets on well with others.*

Give an example of a time when you have taken action to develop a good working relationship with a new colleague or member of staff.

Pick a situation when it was important for you to have a particularly good working relationship with the individual – maybe you were going to be working very closely together, you were going to have to rely on the colleague a lot or the team was very used to working together and it may have been difficult for the member of staff to integrate into this situation. The interviewer will want to assess:

- Why you thought the relationship was an important one.
- What you did to make the person welcome.

- What you did to build a positive working relationship with that person.
- How you adapted your style to suit the individual and the situation.
- What challenges you faced in building this relationship.
- What were the benefits of having a good working relationship.

Describe an occasion when you developed a positive working relationship with a difficult customer or colleague.

Choose an example when there were some significant difficulties at the outset and take this opportunity to demonstrate how your relationship building skills turned the situation around. The interviewer will ask you to describe:

- The tensions in the relationship at the outset.
- Why you wanted to develop a good working relationship with this individual.
- The challenges you faced in seeking to develop a more positive relationship.
- What approach you took to overcoming these challenges.
- The response of the person to this approach.
- What the relationship developed into and how this was beneficial for you and the organisation.

Give an example of a time when you have built a positive working relationship with someone within the organisation but outside of your immediate team.

Relationships with colleagues outside your immediate team can be critical to success and the effective working of an organisation. We often have to rely upon, or work closely with, colleagues from other teams or departments. In asking this question the interviewer will want to assess your understanding of this aspect of relationship building and your approach to working with these colleagues. The interviewer will be interested to hear about:

- Who you were seeking to build a working relationship with.
- Why it was important for you to build this relationship.
- How you understood what he or she might want from the relationship.
- The approach you took to developing this relationship.
- How you evaluated how successful you had been.
- What was the result of building this relationship – the benefits, you yourself, the individual or the organisation.

Example

I was involved in an important new project that would affect most departments but specifically finance. I had had very few dealings with the manager there so this was a good opportunity in which to do so. I needed her skills in order to keep the project online in terms of budget but also her input on how the project should evolve.

Initially I arranged to meet her in the coffee area, very informally, which tends to be my style. I find that people are far more relaxed and open when you do this and any barriers that are there can be broken down easily, not that there were any issues in this case. We were able to strike up a really good rapport. I found out about her interests outside of work coupled with what she specifically wanted to get out of the project.

Through the manager's contribution and dedication we met all targets and were below budget. I really respected her contribution and thanked her for this. We now have a good appreciation of each other's skills and call on each other to help and support in a variety of circumstances, something that didn't happen before. I appreciate her as both a friend and colleague.

> **REMEMBER!**
>
> *Using an example where it wasn't straightforward for you to build a good relationship will demonstrate the competency more strongly than one where they were keen to be your friend anyway.*

Give an example of a time where you have built a good working relationship with an external partner or stakeholder.

Lots of organisations work closely with external partners and stakeholders and the key to a successful outcome is a positive working relationship. Although the relationship is really between two organisations this is often made or broken by individuals that come into contact on a regular basis. The interviewer will want to assess whether or not you understand the critical nature of such a relationship and be provided with evidence of you having successfully done this. You should consider including the following points in your answer:

● Who you were seeking to develop a relationship with.
● Why the relationship was important for your organisation.
● What you had to be sensitive to in building a relationship with an external party.
● What approach you took to building the relationship.
● What the outcome was of taking this approach.
● What you would have done differently.

Managing performance

Managing the performance of the team, and the individuals within it, are key aspects of any supervisor, team leader or manager's role. Employers want to be sure that anyone joining their organisation in one of these roles is clear about this responsibility and has a track record of ensuring that their team performs, so it is important that you are able to talk about this in some detail.

••

Describe an occasion when you have had to manage an individual who was underperforming.

To demonstrate this competency, choose an occasion when you were successful in turning around the situation. The interviewer will want to assess:

- How you approached the situation.
- What you did to understand the reasons for the poor performance.
- How you made it clear to the individual what was expected of that person.
- How you provided support and training to help the individual achieve.
- Whether you developed a plan of action with the individual.
- How you secured the commitment of the individual to improve performance.
- How you monitored progress.
- What the outcome was of working in this way with that person.
- Anything you learnt from this situation.

Describe an occasion when you have had to take someone through the capability/disciplinary process to try to improve their performance.

Although the name and process for this may differ from one organisation to another, the interviewer is essentially looking for evidence of you having experience in using a formal, structured process to manage poor performance or conduct issues. The interviewer will want to hear about:

- What the performance issue was.
- How you gave feedback to the individual – how you prepared for this.
- What steps you took to manage the individual through the formal process.
- What support you had from others, for instance from Human Resources and your line manager.

> **TOP TIP**
>
> Focus your answer on how you sought to improve performance or conduct of the individual rather than just managing that person out of the organisation.

- How you motivated the individual to perform.
- How you monitored progress.
- What outcome you achieved.

Describe an occasion when you have had to manage and motivate an underperforming team to achieve their targets and objectives.

Focus your answer on the motivational aspects of leading the team and be able to give a clear, quantifiable measure of how their performance improved; for example, hit 80 per cent of their targets or met the deadlines required. Include the following points in your answer:

- What the performance issue was.
- How you approached the issue with the team.
- What action you took to motivate your team to achieve.
- How the team responded to your actions.
- What results you achieved.
- What you learnt from this situation.

> **REMEMBER!**
>
> *In questions like this, the interviewer has asked about an underperforming team not an individual within a team.*

Describe the things you do on an ongoing basis to ensure that your team consistently meet agreed targets and objectives.

This question is best answered using the specific approach you have taken with a team – either one you currently manage, or one you have managed in the past. Avoid talking generally, for example, 'I would do this ... I would do that.' It is less convincing and may lead the interviewer to feel that you are talking theoretically and not drawing upon actual experience. The interviewer will want to assess:

- How you motivate the team to achieve.
- How you ensure the team understand their targets and objectives and how well they are performing against them.
- How you review performance as a team and with individuals.
- What you do if the team isn't performing at the level required.
- How you praise and reward the team for achieving.

> **TOP TIP**
>
> As well as describing the actions you have taken as a leader to focus staff on performing, don't forget to also talk about how you have motivated and encouraged them to deliver results.

Using an example to illustrate, describe your approach to celebrating success in the team.

This question is more about the motivational aspects of managing the performance of a team. Positive feedback, praise and recognition for achieving good results are important motivational factors for many people and the interviewer will want to assess whether you understand this and how you go about doing it. Include the following points in your answer:

- Why you believe celebrating success is important.
- Describe a situation when you celebrated success of the team.
- How you celebrated success.
- How you shared any learning derived from this success with other teams or colleagues.
- What impact this recognition of success had upon the team.
- Anything you would have done differently.
- Any feedback you received.

Example

I was responsible for the implementation of a redundancy programme, not a pleasant situation to be in, but none the less important for the success of the organisation. It had been an arduous project for all of those involved, rather 'cloak and dagger' at times, requiring emotional strength and, sometimes, even a sense of humour.

As the project progressed there were long working days so I tried to keep morale up by doing small things, such as ordering pizzas in or getting breakfast delivered.

By the end of the project people were exhausted and emotionally drained. However, we had succeeded in terms of delivering our objectives within the timescales given and to the utmost quality, so my team deserved some form of recognition. Although we couldn't lose sight of the nature of the work we had just undertaken, I felt they needed to let off steam in some way. I asked all of them what they wanted to do in terms of a night out and we decided on a bowling night followed by an informal supper. It was really well received and a joy to see everyone chill out after what was a challenging time.

Feedback was really positive and when we refocused at work after this the team were upbeat and looking forward to getting on with other projects that had taken a back seat. I'm not sure I would have done anything differently, it worked at the time.

Managing change

Change is a consistent factor in organisational life, but something that a lot of people find hard to come to terms with – life is so much easier if things stay the same and you know what to expect. Employers will want to assess both your attitude to change and how well you deal with it at work.

....

Describe an occasion when you have had to be flexible to meet the needs of the organisation.

This question allows you to choose a fairly straightforward, day-to-day example of having to change what you had planned to do and responding to what your manager or colleague needed you to do. Examples might include changing shifts, working late for a few days, helping out another team or taking on some different work. Your answer should include:

- The reason for you needing to be flexible.
- How you needed to be flexible.
- What you did to ensure that your usual work was also done.
- What the benefits were for the organisation or your colleagues.
- What the benefits were for you.
- What you learnt from this situation.

Give an example of a time when you have been involved in a change initiative within the business.

In answering this question you could give an example from a range of change initiatives, such as participating in a change to working practices or systems, a restructure, a change of culture (for example, from sales to service focus), or an office relocation. The interviewer will want to assess:

- Your attitude to the change.
- Your role in the change initiative.
- How you went about fulfilling your role.
- The challenges you encountered.
- How you dealt with these challenges.
- How you supported others going through this change.

REMEMBER!

Although you may have found it difficult to come to terms with change, try to remain positive in your answer – describe what your difficulties were and how you overcame them.

Give an example of when you have led the implementation of change in the workplace.

This question allows you to talk about a major change initiative that you have led in the organisation or how you have implemented change in your team or department. The interviewer will want to assess how you planned the change, won the support of those involved and managed its implementation.
Follow-on questions might include:

- What change were you implementing?
- What factors did you consider in implementing this change?
- How did you plan the change?
- What challenges did you face?
- How did you overcome these challenges?
- What was the outcome of you implementing change in this way?
- What did you learn from this situation?

Describe an occasion when you have supported others through a significant change in the workplace.

The interviewer will want to assess whether you have an understanding of the negative emotions that many individuals have towards change and how you help them to overcome these, feel more secure and come to accept or even welcome the change. Include the following points in your answer:

- What the situation and the change was.
- How you assessed how the individuals impacted by the change were feeling.
- What actions you took to support them.
- How you adapted your approach to suit individual needs.
- What results you achieved by taking these actions.
- What you would have done differently.

REMEMBER!

Although you may not have been successful in changing everyone's attitude towards the situation, choose an example where you were able to help some individuals feel more positive about what was going on and better able to contribute to the process.

Describe an occasion when you were involved in implementing a change at work that you did not agree with.

The interviewer wants to understand how you deal with this kind of situation. Do you demonstrate a negative attitude to the change and try to stop it happening; or do you raise your concerns with more senior people, but ensure that you maintain a positive attitude with your staff and colleagues and encourage them to do what is being asked of them? You should include the following points in your answer:

- What the change was.
- Why you didn't agree with the change.
- How you shared your concerns.
- How you motivated others while feeling negative yourself.
- What you did to support the change.
- What you would have done differently.

Example

When I was working at my last company we were undergoing a company takeover and we became a different company overnight, new name, new branding and refurbished offices. I really didn't agree with the takeover as I didn't think it was right to lose sight of the previous branding and packages that had been available for our customers.

I shared my concerns and views with my manager and the senior team but never with my own team members. I towed the party line and kept focusing on the positive aspects of the takeover, for instance, new uniforms, updated working areas and training. I worked alongside my team members and was there on day one when the new image was launched; they were none the wiser as to how I felt about this.

If I were to do anything differently I think I would have got the people from the other company involved sooner. We held a goodbye and hello party the night before and it would have had better effect if we had all met before this. Although it worked in terms of getting everyone together, it was a little strained at the start.

Creating improvements and innovation

Organisations often place a lot of emphasis upon the need to constantly improve working practices and be innovative at work. The interviewer will want to assess your ability and experience in this area and while few people are truly innovative they will at least expect you to be able to demonstrate what you think about the way you work and seek to find better or quicker ways of completing tasks.

Describe an occasion when you found a better way of completing a task at work.

This could be a fairly straightforward example about a day-to-day task. But choose one where, by changing how you worked, you were able to achieve improved quality of work, reduce time spent on an activity, or work more efficiently with colleagues. Follow-on questions could include:

● What was the task?
● Why did it need improving?
● What did you do to improve how you were working?
● Who else did you involve in making this decision?
● What benefits did you achieve through making these changes?
● What feedback did you receive?

Example

I was responsible for the implementation and running of the commission scheme for our sales force, something not to be taken lightly as this obviously affected individuals' salary. The previous system used a database format but the systems were outdated in terms of formulae and functions. It was also very open to errors, something that happened too often.

I recognised this and highlighted where the changes and improvements needed to happen and made the decision to put these in place. I needed to consult with IT to refine some of the actions I had done and communicated with the head of the sales team to let him know what was happening and how this would impact. However, the final decision was my own.

I implemented the new changes with great success. The launch was very smooth, error rates have decreased significantly; in fact, after six months we had zero errors. We have been able to increase both the speed of turnaround and reduce errors and hence unnecessary time wasting for all involved.

I have received positive feedback from quite a few of the sales force together with the head of the sales team. It was, however, important that I involved IT initially as some of the formulae were too complicated for me and would have taken me so much longer to resolve.

Describe an occasion when you have identified and implemented an improved way of working for yourself and others.

This will require a more complex example than the previous question – a situation where you impacted upon the work of colleagues, the team or even a department. Choose an example where you achieved clear, quantifiable improvements and where you were successful in winning the support of others to the new way of working. Include in your answer the following points:

- What improvement you identified.
- What benefits this improvement would bring for the organisation.
- Who you involved in deciding what the improvement should be.
- How you won the support of colleagues in implementing this improvement.
- What measurable improvements you were able to achieve.
- What you would have done differently.

Describe an occasion when you have encouraged colleagues to challenge what they are doing and identify improved ways of working.

It can be quite a skill to get colleagues and staff to think 'out of the box' and challenge how they go about their work, but one that is increasingly important in the workplace. Think of an example when you have been successful in getting others to do this and the organisation has benefited as a result. Follow-on questions may include:

- How did you encourage colleagues or staff to identify improved ways of working?
- What challenges did you face in getting them to think about this?
- How did you overcome these challenges?
- What changes were implemented and how did these benefit the organisation?
- What did you do to ensure that they would continue to challenge how they worked?
- What did you learn from this situation?

Describe a creative idea that you have come up with in the workplace.

Some organisations need individuals within them who are able to think of creative ideas and bring these to fruition. Choose an example where your idea was accepted, had never been done before and brought tangible benefits to the organisation. It may have been a new product or service, marketing approach, or new way of working. Include the following in your example:

- What your idea was.
- How you came up with the idea.
- How you ensured that the idea was practical.
- What benefits the idea created for the business.
- What you learnt from this situation.

Describe an occasion when you have taken action to foster an entrepreneurial spirit in others.

Again, this will only be a requirement in certain organisations – those that value entrepreneurial ability and are happy to accept the risks that this brings with it. Include in your example how you anticipated and managed risk when you were encouraging others to be entrepreneurial in their approach to work. Follow-on questions may include:

- Why did you want to foster an entrepreneurial spirit in others?
- What did you do to foster this spirit?
- What risks were there in doing this?
- How did you manage these risks?
- What benefits did the organisation gain from you taking this initiative?
- What would you have done differently?

Planning and organising

In questions on planning and organising the interviewer wants to assess the way in which you plan projects and tasks and understand how you prioritise work, allocate resources and overcome any problems that you may encounter in order to meet deadlines.

....

Give an example of how you plan and organise your work so that it is most beneficial and time efficient for your team.

The interviewer is trying to establish how you structure your working day effectively in order to make best use of your time and the team in order to meet deadlines and hit targets. You should include the following points:

- How you approached planning the work.
- How you prioritised tasks in order to make best use of the time for yourself and the team.
- How you allocated resources within the team, for instance, how you looked at strengths and skill of team members.
- How you communicated priorities to the team.
- How successful you feel you were in your planning.

REMEMBER!

You may want to talk through a typical day or week and focus on what you do to plan and prioritise tasks, making best use of the resources within the team, such as identifying strengths of team members to carry out specific duties. Also mention the impact/ implications should priorities end up not being addressed or deadlines met.

Describe an occasion when you have had to translate a strategic business plan into your own department strategy/plan.

The interviewer wants to know how you approach translating the strategy into a more practical plan, relating specifically to your own department and ensure the team understand the requirements. Include in your answer:

- How you approached the translation of the strategy/plan.
- What considerations you took into account when doing this.
- How you ensured your ideas were workable solutions and tied in with the business.
- What input you sought from others.

REMEMBER!

When questions are asked relating to 'strategic' or 'strategy' they want you to focus on the big picture and wider implications affecting the organisation. Give a brief overview of the plan and how you approached translating this. Ensure you keep the practical elements of this to a minimum as they are looking for a strategic answer.

- What resources you needed to deliver the plan.
- How you communicated to your team members.
- How successful you were in translating this plan.
- What feedback you received.
- What you would do differently next time.

Describe an occasion when you have developed and implemented a detailed plan to deliver an important piece of work.

Choose a project or piece of work that you have completed successfully. Give a brief overview of the task and how you planned this, such as referring to how you monitored the task by using Microsoft Project, updated individuals regularly by email, created a clear project plan and shared this with others. Expect to address the following:

- What the project/task was.
- How you approached the planning of this task.
- What methodologies you used to monitor progress; for instance, the project plan.
- How you kept others informed of progress.
- How you adapted the plan to suit the changing needs of the project.
- What problems you faced and how you overcame these.
- How successful you were in delivering the plan.

WARNING!

By choosing an unsuccessful project you may well be digging yourself a hole that is difficult to get out of and that doesn't sell your qualities or paint you in a very good light.

Describe an occasion when you have anticipated issues with a plan and developed and implemented contingency plans.

Focus on the specific issues you anticipated and what actions you took. Pick just one of these that you can talk through in detail and how you dealt with it. You should address the following:

- What the issues were.
- How you became of aware of these; for instance, did someone tell you?.
- What contingencies you put in place and how this addressed the problem.
- What the result was of doing this.
- What the implications would have been if you hadn't addressed this problem. For example, the project deadline was not met and, consequently, the impact on the business or other departments.
- What you learnt from this situation.

Don't:
- Give a long list of problems that you anticipated but are unable to address or talk about in any depth of detail.

Give an example of when you had too much to do and not enough time to complete it in.

This is not a trick question. Interviewers are interested in how you deal with pressurised situations, we have all faced them. Focus on the actions you took. These could include taking a step back and looking at priority items, challenging others on deadlines, seeking assistance or delegating tasks. They are not necessarily looking for you to say you worked until midnight and came in at 7am. Consider highlighting some of the following:

- How the situation arose (was this your own fault or external pressures?).
- How you identified priorities.
- How you dealt with the situation (delegated, negotiated, said no, asked for support).
- How you monitored progress of the tasks.
- How successful you were in meeting deadlines.
- In hindsight, what you could have done differently.

> **REMEMBER!**
>
> *If one of the tasks was still left incomplete, ensure you explain clearly why you chose to leave that one, what the impact was and what you did to deal with this afterwards.*

Give an example of a time when you were unsuccessful in meeting a deadline.

Be honest! We have all done it at some point in time – none of us are perfect. However, pick an example where the implications were not so serious, such as a minor issue that had little impact on the business, team or project, rather than a huge clanger. Think about addressing the following subjects:

- What the situation was. For example, describe the deadline you missed and how this came about.
- The importance of this in relation to the team/department or organisation.
- How you reacted to this, the actions you took.
- How the situation was resolved.
- The impact it had on others, such as the team, department, organisation.
- What you learnt from this situation and how you have used this learning.

Avoid:

- Saying that this has never happened – if this is the case, try to identify the actions you would take in this situation considering the questions detailed to the left.

How do you plan and prioritise your work?

Many people get drawn into giving realms of detail on such issues as to where you place things on your desk, what colours or letters you allocate for urgent items. The interviewer is interested to hear if you have an organised and systematic approach and how you recognise priority items. You could talk about doing something as straightforward as using a system that identifies tasks to be actioned in date order (a 'bring-forward system'), your diary, make lists or using Office Manager. Concentrate on how you plan and how you prioritise.

Avoid:

- Stating that you use a series of Post-it notes across your computer screen – this doesn't describe how organised you are, in fact the opposite, you need reminding constantly of actions.

Example

Generally I organise my work the night before. I like to have a clear head in the morning and know exactly what needs to be done, for who and by when. I briefly look at the tasks in hand and prioritise them in terms of date and urgency, paying attention to deadlines that need to be met in order for me to achieve my target and others to achieve theirs.

During the working day I obviously focus on priorities, but have to be flexible in terms of reacting to urgent tasks that come in during the day. If this does happen, I quickly assess how long they are likely to take and if I have the capacity to do them or not. If not, then I enlist the help of my colleagues or try to renegotiate on the deadline if possible. However, I recognise that sometimes this cannot be.

I also operate a bring-forward system. This ensures that no tasks are put to the bottom of piles or get lost. I am always aware that what I do impacts on the work of others and hence impacts on the level of service we provide our customers.

Leadership

Interviewers want to understand how you lead people – your style, how you interact with team members, how you support them and how you ensure the effectiveness of the team to deliver results.

....

What actions have you taken to ensure that your team works together in the most effective way?

Choose a specific project or task that you can describe in detail. Concentrate on the key words here of 'work together' and 'effective'. You may want to consider addressing some of the following areas:

- How you approached getting the team on board. For instance, negotiate, influence or encourage.
- How you encouraged sharing of information and skills, such as team meetings, shadowing or mentoring of individuals.
- How you allocated tasks – for example, identified skills of team members as some are better at some tasks than others.
- How you regularly updated the team and made them aware of issues and progress.
- How you motivated the team and individual team members.

> **TOP TIP**
>
> When talking about effective team management, you may also want to mention that you have regular updates with individuals to address performance issues. Also describe how you recognise and acknowledge good performance.

Describe an occasion when you have had to work hard to motivate others/the team to achieve their objectives.

The interviewer is looking to establish what methods you adopt and how you adapt your own leadership style to suit the needs of the individuals within the team. Although empathy is important, objectives and tasks need to be achieved for the success of business, so try not to lose sight of this. The interviewer is interested in the following:

- What the situation was.
- How you approached this, such as meeting with the team, offering coaching and mentoring.
- Why you had to motivate the team, what the issues were with people, for instance some individuals were negative, and how you resolved this, recognising the impact on others.

- How you overcame these issues – the actions you took.
- What the end result was.

Describe an occasion when you have led a team/others through a challenging situation.

It is important to focus on how you ensure a team works effectively together, keep them focused on the task in hand despite challenges. The interviewer would like to know the following:

- What the challenges were.
- How you addressed these challenges.
- How the team reacted.
- What you did to address these reactions.
- What the end result was and whether you were satisfied with this.
- If there is anything you would have done differently.

> **REMEMBER!**
>
> *The question focuses on a team rather than dealing with just one individual team member. You could use examples such as redundancy, restructure or challenging timescales or targets.*

Give an example of how you have adapted your style of leadership to meet the needs of others.

The interviewer is looking to understand how flexible you are and how you adapt your leadership/communication style – one size does not fit all. Individuals need handling in different ways; some need more encouragement, some more direction and others to be left to their own devices. Think of a couple of situations and consider covering the following:

- What the situation was.
- How you adapted your style (focus on leadership rather than just communication).
- Why you took the approach you did in terms of your style.
- What the benefits were of this approach.
- What the outcome was.
- How you knew you had met their needs.
- What else you would have done differently.

Example

I was in a situation where I had taken on two new members of staff, both very different in terms of their personality, abilities and learning styles. I recognise the need to adapt to people's different styles as I, for one, like to chat things through, draw diagrams and ask questions and when I was put in a situation where I was left to read information about a new job, I struggled to take it all in and understand it fully.

I spoke with both of them and asked them openly what they wanted to get out of their roles, and how they wanted to tackle their training in terms of job content and understanding the products and services we offered. It was no great surprise that both wanted different approaches.

One individual was happy to be left to read and research information on our intranet and read company brochures, interacting to clarify certain points at infrequent times, while the other wanted more face-to-face interaction, bouncing ideas and asking questions. It was really interesting that at the end of the two-week initial induction period when questioning each of them to establish where they both were in terms of their understanding they were both at a similar level.

This approach was so beneficial as I was able to maintain each of their interest and motivation levels in two very different approaches. Something I will adopt again if needed.

Give an example of a time when you have taken action to ensure the fair and consistent management of people by others.

This question is aimed at managers who manage other managers or team leaders. It is looking to see if you recognise any unfairness, inconsistencies or inappropriate behaviour of managers when dealing with their team members. Do you sweep such issues under the carpet, or do you address these in an open and direct manner and try to understand the issues? What style you adopt? Are you assertive, aggressive or passive? Describe the following:

● What the situation was.
● How it arose – how you learnt of the situation, did you identify this yourself or did someone else bring it to your attention?
● How you approached this with the relevant individuals.
● How they reacted.
● What the outcome was.
● How you monitored the situation thereafter.
● Had you not addressed this, what could have happened?

> **TOP TIP**
>
> On the subject of fair management, you could use examples from redundancy situations, restructuring, a change of management, company takeovers or performance reviews.

Business awareness

This area is directed at identifying your level of general business knowledge and how you keep up to date with specific areas relevant to your job. It also assesses whether or not you consider business issues and activities in terms of cost and profit and your understanding of issues affecting your organisation or industry.

....

Give an example of what you have done to improve your knowledge of the industry or other commercial factors relevant to your role.

Consider the actions you have taken to improve your business understanding; for instance, relevant studies or training course, work shadowing, publications or networking, both internally and externally. This can tell them more about the way you learn and take on board new information – your learning style. Also, how proactive you are in terms of keeping on top of new information. The interviewer will be interested to learn about:

- What you have done to improve your own knowledge and understanding of the business.
- How you approached the learning – perhaps reading up on the internet suits your learning style and fits in with your work/lifestyle.
- What you learnt and give a specific learning point.
- How this has benefited you in your role.

Example

I moved within the organisation from a temporary position into a permanent role within the finance department. However, I realised I had quite a bit of learning to do. As a temporary member I had taken time to understand the organisation I was part of, but not the engineering sector itself. I was going to be involved in making decisions at a more senior level and I needed to be able to contribute more.

I enlisted the help and support of a colleague who I respected and who had vast amounts of engineering experience. Coupled with this, in my own time I researched on the internet, enlisted onto relevant industry journals and attended a couple of seminars relating to engineering in the UK.

These really helped me understand the big picture in terms of where the engineering sector stood within the economy and how we, as an organisation, contributed to this. For instance, we are responsible for 34 per cent of the UK's export of widgets. This enabled me to have a broader view in terms of my role and how finance contributes to this.

Describe what actions you have taken to support others in understanding the wider business/commercial issues affecting their roles.

This is focusing on how you impart your own knowledge and understanding. You may want to talk about how you have translated business information into more easily understandable facts, which directly affect the team or people you work with.

- Why it was important to do this.
- What were the critical issues they needed to understand.
- How you approached supporting others to understand this new information.
- How you ensured understanding; for instance, questioned people.
- How you monitored this to ensure the knowledge was being used effectively.

TOP TIP

For an example of supporting others, think of a specific situation and why it has been beneficial to the individual/team, such as explaining a new legislation, new product, sales targets or industry relevant data.

Describe an occasion when you have considered the costs to the organisation of what you are doing and identified a cheaper way of achieving results.

You need to consider:

- What the occasion was.
- What you did to address the issue, what actions you took.
- What prompted you to do this.
- How you measured this and what the overall savings/benefits were.
- What has been the impact for others/business.
- What you learnt from this.

REMEMBER!

With a question such as this you need to give a tangible outcome, such as what were the overall savings – for example, 15 per cent reduction in product wastage. Be careful not to just pluck an idea out of the air without being able to substantiate the facts.

Give an example of a time when you have identified a way of achieving better business results for the company.

This is directed more towards senior positions such as business leaders. The interviewer wants to assess your commercial awareness and how you have specifically acted to improve the business. Think of a situation where you have introduced a new product, sales target or system. It is important that you explain the points opposite.

- How the situation arose.
- How you approached it.
- How you implemented the changes.
- What the benefits were for the company and how you measured these.
- What risks were involved.
- How you addressed the risks.
- Anything else you could have done.

REMEMBER!

Give evidence that describes how innovative and entrepreneurial you are. Don't just give lots of facts and figures, you need to be able to back this up with what you did to achieve them.

Give an example of a time when you realised you needed to be more aware of business information.

This assesses how aware you are of your own knowledge, its limitations and what actions you take to resolve this. You may want to use an example of a situation where you heard about a new legislation and recognised you knew nothing about it. You could also use examples of first starting within an organisation and realising that there was more information you needed to understand than you originally thought. It is worth addressing the following:

- How you realised you needed to improve your business awareness.
- How you approached this; for instance, reading, internet research, talking with colleagues.
- How difficult it was to understand.
- How beneficial this awareness has been.
- How you have used this information effectively.

TOP TIP

Chose an example that shows you in a positive light – you learnt something and have been able to use it effectively for the benefit of yourself/ team/organisation.

Decision making

Interviewers want you to explain your approach when making decisions. Do you like to consider a wide range of facts and consult with others, or do you shoot from the hip and go with your guts, preferring to make quick decisions?

••

Describe an occasion when you have had to take a complex decision about a work issue.

Focus on the word 'complex', they are not looking for a simple decision.
Use an example that required you to consider a wide range of issues, such as involving people, the business, a strategy or process. Think about how you used information from a variety of sources in order to reach the final decision.
Describe the following:

- What the situation was and why the decision needed to be made.
- What process you adopted to make a decision. Did you involve other people or use facts and figures to support you?
- What made this a complex decision.
- What the end result was.
- Were you happy with the decision you made and is there anything else you would have liked to have known?

> **TOP TIP**
>
> Use an example where you made the right decision.

Using an example, describe how you make a decision at work.

Do you make snap decisions or are you a reflective person, preferring to take your time to consider a range of information before putting your head on the block? Do you involve others or prefer to make decisions alone? The interviewer will want to assess:

- What approach you took when making the decision.
- How you weighed up the pros and cons of the information you had.
- The range of information you considered.
- Who else you involved.
- Were you confident in the final outcome?

Don't:
- Make statements such as, 'I just knew it was right' or, 'It just felt right' – this tells the interviewer nothing about your approach or style to making a successful decision.

Example

I was in a position where I needed to make a decision about which provider to use for our office cleaning services. I got a variety of quotes in from companies and analysed the details against some set criteria, including number of hours, costs per hour, confidentiality policy and feedback from other customers.

From this I then shortlisted three providers and interviewed each of them. This enabled me to gain more evidence in relation to quality of service; for instance, what was 'good' and what was 'excellent' service to the providers. I involved a colleague from purchasing to help me in the final selection decision.

We then made an appointment and were confident in their ability to carry out the service. The providers have now been with us for eight months and we have not had any complaints from staff, only praise.

Describe an occasion when you have supported a colleague/member of staff whose decision has been challenged.

The interviewer wants to establish how you analyse issues with others and how you offer support and guidance. What responsibilities do you take on and how do you empower individuals, giving them the confidence to make a decision again in the future? The interviewer will want to know:

- How you realised you needed to step in and support the individual.
- What support you offered.
- What challenges you faced when dealing with the individual.
- How you helped that person to learn and improve decision making in the future.
- What you learnt from this experience.

Describe an occasion when you have supported a management decision that was unpopular and ensured that it was effectively implemented.

The interviewer wants to establish how you feel about this type of situation, how you detach yourself from the emotional elements involving your staff members or colleagues and how you deal with the follow-on issues as a result. It is important to include the support you offered to the management and how you ensured a united front. Try to include the following elements:

- What the management decision was and how you were involved in this.
- Why this was unpopular with others.
- How you felt about this situation.

- How you ensured its effective implementation.
- How you overcome issues with your staff/colleagues.
- What the end result was.

Give an example of a time when you made an incorrect decision.

We all get it wrong at some point. The interviewer is interested in how you recognise the error of your ways, how you consider the impact this may have and how you correct mistakes. Choose an example that wasn't so drastic your team failed or the company folded. You may be more comfortable using an example outside of work. Consider the following:

- What the situation was that led to the incorrect decision being made.
- How you realised you had got it wrong.
- What the implications were of making the wrong decision.
- The actions you took to put this right.
- Who this involved; for example, did you need to seek assistance or advice from others.
- What you learnt from this experience.

Avoid:

Talking about personal relationship issues – you could start using topics that are not appropriate for the interview situation.

Resilience and tenacity

These questions can be challenging as they are asking you to focus on difficult situations that tested you personally. The interviewer is trying to establish how you work your way through problems and see these through to a suitable conclusion.

....

Give an example of a time when you have encountered a significant setback at work.

The interviewer is looking for you to talk about how you overcome difficulties. Remember to focus on a setback that was significant and use an example from work rather than a personal situation. It is also important to mention what you learnt from this and perhaps how you have applied this learning since. You may want to think about:

- What the situation was and how this arose.
- The approach you took in dealing with this – what you did.
- What support you received/sought from others.
- What considerations you made.
- What the outcome was.
- In hindsight, what you would have done differently.
- What you learnt from this.

TOP TIP

If you are struggling to think of a work-based example relating to a setback, then use a situation from a social experience, but avoid personal topics such as relationship breakups – this is not the time or the place.

Describe an occasion when you have demonstrated a positive attitude in a challenging situation in the workplace to encourage your colleagues.

The interviewer wants to know how you remain positive and if you are able to support and encourage your colleagues through difficult times. You could use examples around change at work resulting from a restructure, redundancy programme, new sales targets or someone leaving the company, which created a large workload for the team. You need to describe:

- What the occasion was.
- Why it was so challenging for you.
- How you encouraged or supported your colleagues.

REMEMBER!

Focus on your specific part in this, and how you contributed to encouraging others – it demonstrates your ability to remain strong and take responsibility.

- Why you needed to do this and how you recognised the need to take action.
- What the impact of your actions was on your colleagues.
- What the end result was.

Describe an occasion when you have supported others who have encountered setbacks or challenges in the workplace.

The interviewer is interested to find out what support you offer to others, how you approach giving this support and how it benefits the individuals. You need to detail how you recognise the need for support and what exactly you do to help people through a situation. The interviewer is interested in assessing:

- What the situation was where support was needed.
- How and why you got involved in this; was this voluntary or did someone ask you for help?
- What difference you made in overcoming the setback/challenge.
- Would you do the same again?
- What feedback you received from the individual(s) you helped.
- What the end result was.

Avoid:
- Describing yourself as the team relationship counsellor.
- Using a work-based challenge or setback.

Give an example of when you have demonstrated resilience in the workplace.

Resilience is the key word here, so don't focus on a small problem that was dealt with quickly. Instead, it may be an issue that lasted a considerable time requiring you to be focused and determined to succeed, such as challenging sales targets for a specific period, working with a limited resource or not having a manager to guide you. The interviewer will want to know:

- An overview of the situation.
- Why you needed to be resilient.
- Why it was important to demonstrate resilience.
- Was there any point you felt like giving up?
- What kept you going – was this support from others or a determination to succeed?
- If you feel you did the right thing.

Example

Following on from a customer review, the company were implementing a new flexible working hour's policy for all staff members in order to meet customer demands. This was obviously good news for our customers, but some members of staff did not take kindly to the fact they were now being asked to work shifts.

I got the team together and listened to their concerns. I understood their feelings, but we needed to move forward and keep in line with other organisations who had already taken the same approach in order to remain competitive and provide the service needed.

There were only a small minority who were opposed to the change. I volunteered myself for the late shifts at the beginning to try to help win their support. I also kept the more positive members involved and their morale eventually influenced those that were more reticent and won them round.

I needed to remain focused and not take this personally. It was a company decision not mine and I managed to remain detached from the emotional side of their issues and focus on the business results, meanwhile maintaining empathy towards their issues and concerns regarding the changes.

Describe a challenging situation from which you feel you learnt valuable lessons.

Although this question is not asking you about a work situation, it is always beneficial to use work if you can. If not, then perhaps you were a member of a society or a club that you could draw on. Try to include positive learning and how you have implemented this. It can demonstrate your ability to take on board information and use it to your, and the organisation's, benefit. Include in your answer:

- How the situation arose.
- What you learnt from this situation.
- How you have applied this learning since and the benefits of this for you and the organisation.

Avoid:
- Sporting related examples such as, 'I didn't train hard enough for my half marathon', or, 'I didn't revise enough for my exams.' This identifies some learning, but it doesn't describe how you can use this learning effectively within an organisation.

Challenge and openness

Within this competency area interviewers are looking for you to describe situations where you have constructively challenged the views/opinions of others, are open and honest with colleagues and encourage discussion and ideas from your team/department.

··

Describe a situation when you have challenged the views of others.

The interviewer is looking to see if you have the confidence and willingness to challenge other people and what approach you take to doing this. Are you aggressive or assertive in your style? Do you ask people lots of difficult questions, which they could not possibly answer to make yourself look good; or do you give people a chance to explain further and gain a better understanding? Consider the following points:

- What the situation was when you felt the need to challenge others.
- How you challenged others, what you said and how you said this.
- How they reacted and how you dealt with these reactions.
- What the overall result of this was.
- Should the situation arise again, would you do/say anything differently?

> **TOP TIP**
>
> Be careful how you explain any challenging situation you were in. It is important that you don't portray yourself as the local troublemaker, challenging people for the sake of making your own voice heard or to make you look good. Challenge can be a positive force in ensuring openness between colleagues at work.

Example

This was when I was attending a team-building event, related to, but outside, of work. We were there to develop ourselves but also to help and support each other. There was one individual who had a particularly strong character and from the very beginning of the day started to dominate the group and assert her opinion on others. She was rather aggressive in her style.

Some less assertive members of the group were beginning to withdraw further from the exercises. I felt someone needed to say something or most of the team were unlikely to benefit from this event. At a coffee break I took this individual to one side and explained the situation from my point of view. At first she was aggressive with her retort, but I remained calm and gave her evidence of her behaviour and how this had impacted on the team. She then backed down, took a step back and listened to others, allowing different people to take the lead and encouraging the quieter members of the group. When the day drew to a close, she stopped me and thanked me for the feedback. Other members of the group thanked me too.
I feel if nothing had been said, most people wouldn't have got anything out of the day.

Describe a situation where others have disagreed with your views.

The interviewer is interested to see how you react and respond to these types of situations. Are you 'fight or flight'? How do you listen to the views of others and how do you try to gain a full understanding of their viewpoint before tackling the challenge? Try to include the following:

TOP TIP

Even if you were unsuccessful in gaining agreement, ensure you focus on the positive outcome or learning from this situation. For example, 'I realised that I had omitted a piece of information or perhaps had not gained the full facts.' Avoid being negative towards the other person or passing blame; be accountable for your own actions.

- How the disagreement arose.
- What the disagreement was about.
- How you handled this disagreement.
- What the challenges were you faced.
- Why it was important for you to do this.
- How successful you were in gaining their agreement and resolving the disagreement.
- Would you have done anything differently?

Describe a situation where you have disagreed with the views or actions of others.

Use an example that avoids describing yourself as someone who likes the sound of their own voice and disagreeing with trivial and meaningless things. Use a situation that had significant impact on yourself or others. Try to include the following:

- How this disagreement came about.
- Why you disagreed with the person/people.
- How you told them you disagreed with them.
- What the impact was of this on yourself and others.
- How they reacted to your challenging them.
- What the end result was.

Give an example of when you have demonstrated openness at work.

The interviewer is trying to establish how upfront and honest you are at work. Do you tend to accept issues and go with the flow, even if you don't agree, or are you willing to let others know how you feel in an open and constructive manner? It could be you don't feel comfortable about how a situation has been handled by a colleague or perhaps don't understand the point of a new process you have been asked to follow. The interviewer is interested in the following detail:

- How the situation arose where you needed to share your views and be open with colleagues.
- Why you felt the need to address this situation.
- How you approached this with others – did you speak with people individually or did you talk as a team?
- Why this was important for you to do.
- Would you do the same again?
- What the benefits were for addressing the situation when you did.

Describe an occasion when you have taken action to encourage an open environment in the workplace where people feel able to challenge one another.

To illustrate this point, you need to identify how you encourage people to share their views and opinions openly, without them feeling uncomfortable. The interviewer will want to establish if you recognise that everyone is entitled to an opinion, that some people feel more comfortable than others explaining their thoughts and ideas, and how you recognise and address this. Some ideas for consideration are:

- Why it was important for people to be open in this situation.
- How you approached this situation, such as a team meeting, written communication.
- Why you took this approach.
- How you ensured understanding of any issues that arose.
- What the outcome was.
- What you learnt from this.
- What else you would/could have done.

Problem solving

The interviewer is trying to establish your approach and style to solving problems. Do you focus on the opinions of others and would rather speak with people to resolve issues, or do you like to have a wide range of facts, figures and data available? Or perhaps you use a bit of both?

· ·

Give an example of a time when you have had to analyse information in order to find a solution to a problem.

The interviewer wants to establish what types of information you consider and how you make connections between certain pieces of data in order to resolve problems. They are interested in:

- What the information was you had to analyse.
- How you approached this analysis.
- How you recognised the links across information.
- Whether you consulted with anyone else to discuss a possible solution and why.
- What the end result was – were you successful in finding a solution?
- Should the situation arise again, what you would have done differently.

> **TOP TIP**
>
> Keep your example logical and focused – and have a clear, positive outcome.

Example

I was given my monthly data statistics, which made reference to the fact that my department had not hit target by 25 per cent. I was surprised and didn't feel this was accurate as I had been keeping a rough record myself. A number of things crossed my mind, was it that the team was being lazy as I had been out of the office for a few days? Perhaps they were not making best use of the time available? Were they ignoring the targets or was there an error within the data?

I went back through all of the relevant information, breaking down the statistics into tasks and individuals. I also compared this to my own stats. I realised that there were two individuals who had been inputting the data incorrectly – we were actually 25 per cent ahead of target! I spoke with them both and identified a training need.

The very next day we went through the various different systems and data collection methods. They both recognised where things had gone wrong and the situation was resolved. I learnt never to just take information on face value and to always look 'behind the numbers' to identify the issues. If the situation should arise again, I would look at the wider issues around the data not just the black and white information.

Describe a situation when you have had to solve a difficult problem.

What seems like a relatively straightforward question could lead into all sorts of issues. Don't get too detailed and complicated in describing this. Keep focused on the problem, your approach and the end result. Stick to the following points:

- What the problem was and how it arose.
- Why this was so difficult to resolve.
- What approach you took to resolve this problem.
- Did you have to consult with others or handle it on your own?
- How successful you were in achieving an outcome.
- Is there anything else you would have done differently?

> **REMEMBER!**
>
> *Describe clearly the information you gathered and analysed to solve this difficult problem and why it was important to consider that information.*

Describe an occasion when you have worked with others to solve a problem at work.

In this question the interviewer is not interested in whether or not you can save the planet single handedly, but in how you work with others to solve a problem, what contribution you make and how you take on board the ideas of others. In your answer, ensure you describe how you work towards a common goal. You may want to consider the following:

- What the problem was that you and others faced.
- How you worked with others in tackling the issues. Did you do this together or have individual roles?
- What your contribution was and what difference you made to solving the problem.
- What challenges you faced while trying to solve the problem.
- How you overcame these challenges.
- What the end result was.

Don't:
- Be led down the route of talking about 'we'. This question is asking how you work with others, so describe your specific contribution.

Give an example of a time when you were unable to solve a problem.

This is not a trick question – we cannot be successful at resolving every single issue! Choose an example that had limited impact on others or the organisation. The interviewer is interested to assess if you understand why you were unsuccessful and what you learnt from this situation. The interviewer will focus on the following:

- What the problem was.
- What approach you took to seeking to resolve it.
- Why you were not successful in achieving a positive outcome.
- What the impact of this was on you, the team or the organisation.
- What you learnt from this situation and if you have been able to put this learning into practice since.

Describe an occasion when you have had to solve a problem alone at work.

The interviewer is interested in understanding the approach you take to problem solving if you are unable to consult with colleagues – can you think on your feet, generate a number of solutions to the problem and then select the right course of action? Cover the following points:

- Why you had to solve the problem alone.
- What the benefits/drawbacks are of working in this way.
- What approach you took to solving the problem.
- What the outcome was and what you learnt from this situation.

Competency based questions

Company vision

This section is mainly focused towards more senior posts, those responsible for contributing at a strategic level. The interviewer wants to see how committed and determined you are to developing a company vision or culture and how you approach communicating this to others – helping them to understand their role in bringing it to life.

....

Give an example of how you ensure you have a good understanding of the organisation's goals and vision.

The best way to tackle this is to demonstrate how you take a proactive approach in ensuring you understand the company's vision and long-term goals. They are assessing how you ensure you understand the big picture/wider issues affecting an organisation. Identify the following:

● What led to you taking action – how you became aware of the need to do this.
● Why you needed to have a good understanding of the organisation's goals and vision.
● What approach you took and how beneficial this approach was.
● How you ensured your own understanding was correct.

Example

The situation arose in my first senior level appointment. I recognised instantly the need to get up to speed with the company issues in terms of their five-year strategic plan, how my role and my department contributed to this and what actions I needed to take. I had a broad overview, but needed to understand far more about the strategic elements to ensure I could contribute effectively and add value to the senior team.

> **TOP TIP**
>
> An example of showing a good understanding of a company's goals and vision could include when you first started at a company or when the organisation changed its vision or way of working.

I attended all of the relevant senior management meetings and liaised closely with a specific member of the senior team who I had worked with previously. Through attending meetings, reading information and asking questions I was quickly able to prioritise the projects within my team, something my predecessor had lost sight of.

I was then able to meet with my team and communicate where our focus was going to be and give them more support and direction. It was also an opportunity to clarify any misunderstandings from their previous manager. This approach was beneficial in terms of me gaining an understanding from the top and then being able to break this down into how our departmental plan tied in with the company's goals and vision.

Describe an occasion when you took action to ensure that company values were lived out.

The interviewer is interested to see what contribution you have made to this. It could be you are a manager and ensure your team/department understands the vision – perhaps they had lost sight of the end goal and you needed to refocus them on the bigger picture. They also want to see that you have a personal commitment and determination to ensure that the company values are adhered to. Consider the following:

- How you became aware of the need to take action.
- How you approached the situation.
- The challenges you faced and how you overcame these.
- How you ensured understanding by all those involved.
- What the end result was.

Give an example of when you have contributed towards the development of the organisation's vision and goals.

The interviewer is interested to see what input you have had at this strategic level and explore the role you have had in the development of the organisation's overall aims. They will want to know the following:

- What contribution you made to the development of the vision and goals.
- How you approached this.
- How you kept focused on the big picture and wider issues rather than what your own department needed.
- What problems you faced and how you overcame these.
- What the overall benefits were of doing this.

Describe an occasion when you have acted as an ambassador for the organisation and enhanced others' views of the company.

Pay attention to why you were chosen as the ambassador, why it was important to do this and how you enhanced the views of others. In preparation, consider the points given overleaf.

> For me, an interviewee has to have a real desire to work for the company – to know what makes us stand out from our competitors and to not be afraid to be critical about what we do well, and how we can improve. Those with rose-tinted spectacles need not apply!
>
> MANDY FERRIES, HEAD OF PERSONNEL AND TRAINING, JD WETHERSPOON PLC

TOP TIP

Identify a situation that you were fully bought into and that you can communicate with energy and passion. It is very easy to identify candidates who don't fully believe in what they are saying.

- What the situation was and how this arose.
- Why you think you were chosen to act as an ambassador and how this made you feel.
- What particular challenges you faced.
- What you did to portray a positive image of your organisation in the minds of others.
- How you measured success.
- What feedback you received.

Give an example of how you have brought the corporate vision to life for others, helping them to understand and support the long-term aims of the organisation.

The interviewer wants to assess how you ensure understanding and how you demonstrate your commitment to ensure others are brought in and share the company's vision. They will be interested to hear about how you make it understandable for others, and whether you are compelling in selling the vision or do you lack confidence in what it might achieve? The interviewer is likely to focus on the following:

> ## TOP TIP
> The manner in which you deliver your answer can say a lot about your commitment and enthusiasm for the situation.

- How you brought the vision to life for others.
- What challenges you faced and what you did to address these.
- How you remained positive throughout and how difficult this was.
- If there were any parts of the vision you didn't agree with.
- How you overcame this issue.
- How you ensured understanding of others regarding the vision.
- What you would do differently.

Give an example of a time when you were involved in the promotion of a new brand.

The interviewer is looking to see how you involve yourself and how you approached the promotional aspects. Depending on the role you are applying for, they may want to see how creative and innovative you are in your approach to promoting products – for instance, marketing skills. They will like to know more and gain understanding in:

- What the brand was and how involved you were in the development of this.
- What you contributed in terms of the promotional aspects.
- How you approached this and how beneficial your contribution was.
- What difference you made to the success of this.

Integrity

Ethics and values play a large part in organisational life for many companies. The interviewer is seeking to establish how you ensure you work with integrity, what actions you take to promote ethical conduct and if you adopt an unbiased approach towards others. It is a good idea to research a company's ethical approach and culture from their website or company literature as this can help steer you in the right direction if faced with questions on this subject.

....

Describe an occasion when you have had to maintain confidentiality about something in the workplace.

The interviewer is looking to understand if, and when, you believe it is important to maintain confidentiality – you may want to be discrete within the example you choose. For example, don't mention any names and give an overview of the situation. You need to be able to explain the situation and why it was important to maintain confidentiality. This also demonstrates your ability to be professional and take responsibility. You can expect to provide information around:

- What the situation was and how this came to your attention.
- How you realised the need to be confidential – what the impact would be if you didn't.
- How you felt throughout this. Were your own values being challenged?

Example

It was a situation involving a colleague, someone within my team. He spoke to me in confidence and told me that he was undergoing tests for a serious illness and although he appeared OK, he was really quite poorly.

I was comfortable keeping the confidence initially, but after a couple of weeks his work was beginning to slacken and his attendance was dropping; for instance, he was coming in late and leaving early. I felt like I was in between a rock and a hard place as other members of the team had obviously started to notice and comments were being made, which was affecting the morale of the team.

I encouraged him to speak with our team leader to explain the situation but he wanted to wait until he had confirmation of his illness. I felt really awkward, but I continued to respect his decision not to tell anyone else.

I feel I did the right thing. The individual was very ill and eventually he was able to tell our team leader and the rest of the team about his difficult situation. He thanked me afterwards for keeping the situation to myself and apologised to me as he recognised this had been a difficult situation.

Describe an occasion when you identified that someone was acting in an unethical manner at work.

The interviewer wants to establish if you have the confidence to tackle issues where you feel people are acting in an unprofessional manner and if are you willing to take on the responsibility or approach others for assistance and advice. They are looking for you to explain:

- What the situation was.
- Why the behaviour was unethical and its potential impact.
- What options you considered and the actions you took to address this situation.
- What challenges you faced and how you dealt with these.
- What the end result was.

> ## WARNING!
> Try to keep this as factual as possible rather than stating opinions – this can lead to all sorts of issues and become a very emotive answer.

Describe the actions you have taken to ensure ethical conduct among others in the workplace.

The interviewer is looking to see if you are willing to take the responsibility to ensure that others understand issues relating to ethical practices. Do you recognise the impact of unethical conduct on others, or the organisation, and how strongly do you feel about this? Describe the following:

- What the situation surrounding ethical conduct was.
- Why you felt the need to act.
- How you approached this situation.
- Why you approached it in this manner.
- Why it was important to address the unethical conduct issue.
- What the outcome was.

Give an example of when you feel you have acted with integrity in the workplace and encouraged others to do the same.

The interviewer wants to know how you approach such situations and how you act in the best interest for an individual, the team or the company. Are you able to relate this to the company culture and values? Consider covering the following points:

- What the occasion was where you acted with integrity.
- Why you felt you had to act that way and what you did.

- The implications should you not have taken this action.
- How you encouraged others to act with integrity.
- What the overall outcome was.
- What you learnt for this situation.

Avoid:
- Stating, 'I do this all the time', or, 'it felt right.' This tells the interviewer very little about your understanding of ethical issues.

Describe a time when you have challenged others who you felt were acting without integrity.

This can be a big issue within organisations, especially at a more senior level. It is important that people are not seen to be turning a blind eye or ignoring situations that could potentially get out of hand and cause significant damage to individuals, teams and the overall business. The interviewer is looking for you to highlight the following:

- What the situation was and how it arose.
- Why you felt the need to challenge this.
- What the actions were you took.
- What the impact could have been had you not acted on this.
- What difference you made to others.
- Would you do the same thing again?
- What you learnt from this situation.

Respecting equality and diversity

Equality and diversity are high on many organisations' agendas. The interviewer is seeking to establish how you ensure equality and diversity within the workplace and what actions you take to promote such practices, or to challenge malpractices. They also want to assess whether or not you recognise inconsistencies between what people say or do regarding equality and diversity – do you challenge them and seek to act as a positive role model through your own behaviour?

Describe an occasion when you have had to deal with a customer/colleague in a culturally sensitive manner.

It is important to describe the approach you took and why you felt the need to act, the outcome and potential issues should the situation not be dealt with properly. You could consider examples relating to understanding, such as communicating with someone where English is not their first language, or perhaps explaining a specific process and why it needs to be adhered to. Consider the following:

● What the occasion was and how it arose.
● How you approached this sensitive issue.
● Why you acted on this in the way you did.
● What the final outcome was.
● Would you have done anything differently?

Avoid:
● Culturally sensitive does not necessarily mean religious issues – it may be safer to steer clear of such examples as you may inadvertently get yourself into difficult ground.

Describe an occasion when you have had to accommodate the cultural views of others at work.

The interviewer wants to know what you do to overcome such difficulties and if you take action to understand the cultural views of others to better appreciate their point of view, not just taking these views at face value. We would recommend choosing an example that would address any of the points opposite.

> **WARNING!**
>
> This could potentially be a sensitive area and it is important to avoid topics such as religion and politics in the interview.

- What it was that was difficult for you to respect.
- What you did to overcome this.
- What you learnt by doing this.

Describe an occasion when you have been aware of inappropriate behaviour by a colleague/customer towards somebody else.

The interviewer is trying to identify if you have the confidence to take responsibility for these situations and address them, or do you just sit back and ignore it, hoping it will go away? It is also important to demonstrate how you approach these situations. Are you a 'bull in a china shop' or do you try to establish the full facts before jumping to conclusions? The interviewer will want to know the following:

- How the situation arose and you became aware of it.
- The actions you took to address the inappropriate behaviour.
- Why you thought it important to act on this behaviour.
- How the person reacted to you.
- What the end result was.
- What the implications would have been if you hadn't taken action.

Describe an occasion when you have challenged the behaviour of others in the workplace to ensure that they show respect for the opinions, circumstances and views of others.

Focus on why you feel the need to challenge others and how you follow through these situations to ensure people show respect, how you gain agreement and ensure they understand the consequences for not doing so. It is key to be able to identify the bigger picture and help others understand the consequences of their actions. Expect to explain the following:

- What the issue was.
- The actions you took to address the behavioural issues.
- How you helped them to understand the views, concerns or circumstances of others.
- How you encouraged them to show respect to others.
- How you monitored events afterwards.
- The impact should you not have stepped in.

> **REMEMBER!**
>
> *Identify what you actually did and keep it factual rather than focus on heresay.*

Describe an occasion when you have taken action to ensure that others in the organisation are behaving so they show they are valuing and working effectively with diversity.

The interviewer wants to know what you do when people are pushing the boundaries of equality and diversity. Are you willing to challenge and take responsibility for such issues and ensure others work within policies and procedures? Are you able to gain agreement from others to ensure they value this or do you just pay lip service to it? Consider addressing the following:

● Give an overview of the situation and how this arose.
● What issues you identified.
● How you ensured diversity was understood and valued by others.
● How you followed this up afterwards. For instance, did you meet with others or keep any eye on the situation from a distance.
● What the benefits were of taking action when you did.

Giving an example to illustrate, describe how you feel that equality and diversity should be promoted in the workplace.

A good way of answering this question would be to talk generally about your approach to ensuring you are up to date with the organisation's diversity and equality policy and how you raise awareness of this among your colleagues or team. You may then want to explain a situation where you have actively promoted equality and diversity in the workplace – examples might include a recruitment initiative or a training or briefing session you have run. Look at including in your answer:

● The action you took.
● Why you believed it was important to do this.
● What the benefits were of taking this action.

Example

I ensure that people treat each other with respect. I question people's behaviour should I not feel they are acting appropriately, but first establish if they understand the organisation's policy relating to this area. I have run short training sessions in our team briefings to ensure that everyone is up to date with what the company expects of them in this area. If such areas are not addressed immediately, they can escalate, causing unnecessary upset to others.

11 It's your turn

 **Question time**

Question time

As the interview draws to a close the interviewer asks, 'Do you have any questions for us?', a question that many dread and others can't wait to get started on. This chapter provides a range of questions that you could ask to help you find out what you want to know together with guidance on the types of question to avoid asking at this stage of the selection process.

Do I have to ask questions?

It is not compulsory to ask questions, the interviewers may have given you a good understanding of the key issues that you wanted to know about as part of the discussion you had in the interview. It does, however, create a positive impression in the interviewer's mind if you have at least a couple of questions, showing you are interested in the job and in finding out more about it.

What questions should I ask?

The interview should be seen as a two-way process. It is as much about you deciding whether they are the kind of organisation or people you would like to work with, so make the most of the opportunity to ask a few questions. Think about what aspects of the company, job, benefits or opportunities are important for you to understand more about in order to make a decision about your future if you are successful in being offered a job. Having identified what these are, look through the suggested questions below and pick out those that you feel best suit your needs. Write these down to take into the interview – the chances are that in the excitement of the interview you won't remember them all.

The company
● What is it like working for this company?
● How long have you been employed with this company?
● What challenges do you feel this company faces over the next two years?
● What changes have you seen in the organisation since you have been here?

The job
● What induction is available?
● What skills and qualities do you believe are important for this role?
● What are some of your major projects currently being undertaken?
● How much teamwork is involved in the role?
● How much time is spent working alone on projects?

11

- How much autonomy will I be given?
- How much contact initially am I likely to have with customers/clients?
- In which location is this role undertaken?
- How much travel will be involved?
- How many people are there in the team?
- How many people will I have direct responsibility for?
- Could you please describe a typical day/week for me?
- Is there anything in my skills/experience that concerns you?
- Is there anything else I can tell you about my suitability for this role?
- Is there anything I have said today that concerns you?
- Is there anything I have not said that I can expand on?
- Why has the position become vacant?
- How many posts are there?

Training and development
- What training is available for this role?
- What support is given for further qualifications?

Career progression
- What are the opportunities for promotion?
- Do you promote internally where possible?
- Are there likely to be any overseas opportunities in the future?

Salary and benefits
- Can you please confirm the salary and benefits package?
- You mention flexible benefits, what do you mean by this, how are these broken down?
- Do you offer a relocation package?
- How often are the salary reviews conducted?
- Do you offer childcare facilities?
- What onsite facilities do you have? For example, gym, restaurant, kitchen, showers?
- What pension scheme do you run?
- How soon could I become a member of the pension scheme?
- What sort of car would I get as part of the car scheme?
- How many days' holiday would I get?

General information
- What appraisal process do you have in place?
- If I were successful in being offered this job, could I come in to meet colleagues and have a look around the offices before the first day?

- Is there a probationary period?
- What is the dress code for your organisation?
- I have x disability. How will you accommodate my needs?

What happens next?
- When are you looking for someone to start in this role?
- When will I be advised about the result from this interview?
- How will you contact me after this interview?
- Can I just check with you that you have my correct details as I have changed my telephone number/moved address recently?
- Is there feedback available from this interview?
- How can I obtain feedback from you?

Questions to avoid asking

In order to maintain a positive impression of yourself in the mind of the interviewer, there are some questions you just shouldn't ask.

Questions about the number of candidates make you appear as though you are calculating your chances – it is really irrelevant how many people are being interviewed. If you are the best candidate for the job, you will be offered it; if you are not right for the job, you won't – regardless of whether there were ten or 110 applicants.

Many sales people feel it demonstrates that they can close a sale if they ask, 'Have I got the job?' No experienced or professional interviewer is going to make a decision until they have seen all the candidates – if they feel they are in a position to offer you the job there and then, they will do so, but you are not going to encourage them to do this by asking them.

Questions you should avoid asking
- How many people applied for the job?
- How many people are you interviewing for the job?
- Do you think I have performed well enough at this interview to be offered the job?
- Will you confirm to the Job Centre that I have attended for this interview?
- How do you think I have performed at this interview?
- Have I got the job?
- When can I start?
- How many statutory sick days am I entitled to?
- Can I travel first class wherever I go?

> **TOP TIP**
>
> Avoid asking too many questions at the close of an interview – the interviewers are likely to be on a tight time schedule to see other candidates so be sensitive to this. Three or four questions should suffice.

12 Assessment centres

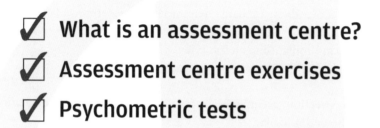

☑ **What is an assessment centre?**

☑ **Assessment centre exercises**

☑ **Psychometric tests**

What is an assessment centre?

Assessment centres are increasingly common as a selection method and are being used by more and more employers to help them choose the right people for their organisation. Public Sector organisations or those carrying out volume recruitment are particularly likely to use this approach to selection. This chapter explains what assessment centres are, why they are used and gives detailed guidance on the types of exercise or test you may be asked to complete and how to approach completing these.

An assessment centre is essentially the use of a range of exercises or assessment methods rather than just an interview. The exercises will allow candidates to demonstrate the skills required in the role and the exercises are often based on the job itself, simulating activities or situations that you would find yourself in. Assessment centres usually use a group of assessors who will observe, record and assess the behaviour of candidates and make decisions against predetermined selection criteria. Love them or hate them, assessment centres are becoming increasingly popular with employers as they provide a far more robust and reliable process than simply using an interview.

In summary, assessment centres:

- Use multiple selection techniques, such as group exercise, presentation, analysis exercise and role play.
- Use a group of assessors with selection decisions made on a group basis.
- Are based on aspects of the job the person will be required to carry out.
- Allow assessments to be made of candidates interacting with other people rather than just working alone.
- Are behaviourally based, what you see someone doing/how they do it.

It is good practice for organisations to offer feedback to candidates after an assessment centre, relating to their performance across the different exercises. This is something that can generally be obtained over the phone or face to face, regardless of whether you are successful or not.

The assessment centre is likely to be the final phase of the recruitment process, although this is dependent upon the company processes and you may well be asked to attend a final stage interview with the recruiting manager.

The benefits of using assessment centres

These are twofold. For the organisation, assessment centres:

- Are more objective and so provide a fairer selection process.
- Are the strongest predictor of future performance in the role.
- Get a rounded picture of an individual, seeing how that person works in a variety of situations.
- Focus on specific competencies needed for the role.
- Are thorough, avoiding reliance on one exercise or one opinion.
- Have a range of assessors, which helps achieve a balanced picture of a candidate's overall skill level and style of working.
- Allow a variety of managers or staff to become involved in assessing candidates and making the selection decision. This will ensure they are committed to the decisions made and the new staff that will join the organisation as a result.
- Allow assessors to spend more time with candidates than in a simple interview and sell their organisation to them.

For you, the candidate:

- You can demonstrate skills in a variety of situations. We are all good at different things, some people do well in interviews others prefer to do something more practical; for instance, conduct a telephone conversation with a customer. An assessment centre usually means there is something in there that everyone will feel they can excel at.
- You have the opportunity to demonstrate skills you may not use in your current role. By putting you in practical situations it is possible to see how you would approach work that you have not yet had the opportunity to be involved in. This can be particularly useful when identifying people for promotion or identifying development needs.
- You can learn about your strengths and or development needs. By being placed in a variety of situations over a short time you often learn a lot about yourself, the things you enjoy or don't enjoy, and where your strengths or development needs lie.
- An assessment centre is often a good way for you to find out more about the company. You get to spend time with people in the business and gain a better understanding if it is the kind of place you would like to work and the sort of people you would like to work with.

TOP TIP

At an assessment centre make good use of any down time. For example, during coffee and lunch speak with as many people as possible from the company who are at the centre and ask any questions you may have.

- Your performance is not dependent upon one exercise or activity. If you feel you have not done your best in one of the activities, you have the opportunity to put it behind you and put 100 per cent into the next session to show your true skills and qualities.

What are assessors looking for?

Assessors look for two main things:

- Your performance against agreed selection criteria for the role.
- You to be yourself.

When participating in an assessment centre always keep in mind the criteria that you are being assessed against – the key skills and qualities for the role. These will be stated in the original job advertisement, the invitation to attend the centre or, sometimes, even in the introduction to each exercise.

As you complete each exercise it can be useful to check whether or not you have demonstrated these key skills in that exercise – for example, it can be easy to focus upon analysis or problem solving when completing an analysis exercise but forget to demonstrate your people skills. Likewise, in a group exercise candidates can often get carried away working effectively with colleagues and forget that there is actually a task to achieve in a tight timescale.

Although some candidates feel, at first, that the assessment centre is a false environment, it is important that you are yourself – you are not being required to act. Once you get into each of the exercises, that feeling will fade and you will become absorbed in completing the activities as requested.

Assessment centre exercises

Assessment centres can include any of the following and run for as little as half a day to one or two days assessment. Below is an indication of the range of different assessment exercises you can expect to undertake:

- Group
- Written
- Analysis
- In-tray or in-basket
- Case study
- Fact-find
- Presentation
- Role play/interactive or simulation
- Scheduling
- Interview
- Psychometric tests (see pages 238–44)

At the end of most exercises you will be given a form to complete that asks you to reflect on the exercise you have just completed. Typically it will include questions such as:

- How did you find the exercise?
- How did you approach the exercise?
- Were you happy with the outcome?
- Is there anything you would do differently, and why?

Don't treat this as a paper exercise. Your assessors will use this information to give them valuable information about your ability to evaluate your performance and your understanding of the exercise. For instance, if there is something you think you could have done differently, then highlight what you would have done in this form. Be honest, if you think you did a poor job, then say so.

Group exercises

Group or team exercises are where a group of candidates are given some information to work with and asked to work together to reach a decision, work out an answer or construct an item from materials provided. There are often no right or wrong answers, assessors are interested in the way you work with others and conduct yourself in a group or team situation. Group exercises are either non-assigned role or assigned role discussions.

Non-assigned role group discussion

Individuals are given the same brief of information, which in most cases consist of a range of different work-related issues requiring action or discussion where a decision or course of action needs to be agreed with all group members. In some cases, individual preparation time is given if the exercise is more complex.

Assigned role group discussion

Each individual within the group is given a different brief of information. You may each be representing a different area of the business and have competing interests, needing to make a decision that will benefit not only your own area or department but the overall good of the company.

A group discussion often begins with some preparation time. As a participant you will be given from 5 to 15 minutes to read through some information, on your own, in order to make notes and gain an understanding of the exercise and what you need to do before the discussion actually starts. The discussion itself can range from 15 minutes to one hour and is timed by the assessors. Whether or not you have reached a conclusion, the discussion will be stopped after the agreed time, so it can be important to keep an eye on the time as the discussion progresses.

In groupd exercises, participants are usually seated around a table with their brief of information, pen and paper. It is very rare that a chair for the discussion will be appointed; in fact, most assessors want to see how people work together as a group. Your fellow candidates will be seated at the table with you and the assessors positioned around the room at a distance from the candidates. The assessors will be taking notes and assessing both what you say and your behaviour; for instance, your non-verbal behaviours. You need to ignore they are there: this is easier than it sounds once you have got into the discussion with your fellow candidates. There will usually be four to six people in a group exercise.

> A candidate's cultural fit is just as important as their ability to do the job. Therefore, be yourself at the interview. This will help the recruiting manager to understand whether your personality fits and whether you are the perfect candidate. Being yourself will also give the candidate the ability to test their fit with the organisation. You don't want to be in the situation where you leave a job and find that two months later you don't fit into your new role.
>
> CHRIS CLARK, HR MANAGER, MAZDA MOTORS UK

TOP TIPS

- It is very difficult to prepare for a group exercise.
- Be yourself.
- Try to involve everyone in the group, especially quieter members.
- Try not to talk over others.
- If you agree to be the timekeeper, carry it through.
- If you agree to take notes for the group, then be prepared to recap on these.
- If you make the decision to write on the flipchart, be careful not to take yourself out of the discussion.
- Ensure you make eye contact with the all of the group when you are speaking.
- Ensure you actively listen to others; for example, nod or smile in agreement.
- Those who shout loudest in a group exercise don't necessarily win.
- You need to contribute more than just saying, 'That's a good idea'; have some ideas of your own.
- Make notes yourself as this will help you keep track of the discussion.

Another form of group exercise is where individuals work together as a group to build or make something or work on a practical problem solving exercise. This is more likely to be the case in industries such as engineering.

Written exercises

Written exercises are completed individually and are timed. You are given a range of information and asked to either write a response or make a recommendation based upon this information. This can be anything from a letter of complaint from a customer to writing a briefing note for your manager. You may have to write this by hand or type it into a computer.

Generally assessors are looking for a range of information including how you present information, grammar and spelling. Depending upon the nature of the exercise, they could be looking for evidence around customer service, empathy, problem solving and decision making.

These exercises are typically anything from 30 minutes to one hour in length.

TOP TIPS

- Ensure that you fully understand what you have to do before you start. If you don't, then ask.
- Ensure you read through the exercise brief before putting pen to paper.
- Make brief notes on rough paper first.
- Allow enough time to complete the exercise.
- Read through what you have done afterwards if you have enough time.

Analysis exercises

In this type of written exercise you are given a range of information, usually both verbal and numeric, relating to specific work-related scenarios. Information is presented in a variety of formats, including written text, tables, graphs, spreadsheets and charts. You will be required to analyse this information and either produce a report or make a presentation detailing your recommendations, or sometimes both. Analysis exercises are completed on an individual basis.

Scenarios given cover a variety of situations from assuming the role of a manager of a department and identifying how performance can be improved, to taking the role of an external consultant and looking at how best to implement a company merger. The assessors are not only looking for you to make recommendations and identify issues, but look at some of the tenuous links that may be incorporated and if you have included a range of issues. For instance, don't just concentrate on making maximum profit but look at the impact on the staff morale.

These exercises can be challenging as you are presented with a large amount of information and only have a relatively short amount of time to complete them in. Typically they last from 45 minutes to two hours depending upon how much information is being analysed.

In-tray or in-basket

These exercises are completed on an individual basis and taken under timed conditions. They are a good way of identifying how you are likely to deal with a range of different information, how you plan and organise your time, and whether or not you can pick up information quickly in order to make informed decisions.

A likely scenario is you will be given the in-tray or in-basket of a predecessor, which must be managed, arranged, issues resolved and decisions made within a set period of time. The contents will be typical of items found

TOP TIPS

- If you don't understand anything, then ask prior to the exercise starting.
- Make a note of the specific actions you are being asked to address.
- Read through the information first, using a highlighter to pick out the key points.
- Pace yourself, allocate yourself a certain amount of time to read the information through.
- Make notes, ensuring that you leave enough time to plan your answer and write your report.
- Consider the full range of information – don't just focus on one area.
- Make a note of the finish time of the exercise – and keep an eye on the time as you work.

REMEMBER!

A common mistake when completing written, analysis and in-tray exercises is to spend too much time reading through the information in great detail and not leaving enough time to complete the final report and give recommendations. Don't let that be you – the assessors cannot assess the part of your answer that is left in your head.

12

TOP TIPS

- If you are in any doubt of what you need to do, ask before the exercise starts.
- Make sure you read through everything before taking any action.
- If you recognise items are linked to others, place them physically together or make a note to remind yourself of this.
- Don't just make a quick note on the item itself; where possible, write a letter or response in full.
- If you are asked to write a response, do it. Don't just make a note on the item saying 'response needed'.
- Keep an eye on the time as it passes very quickly in these exercises.
- Clip items together once you have completed the necessary action or response.
- If you can, arrange the items in order of importance, for instance as you would like someone to pick them up and deal with them.
- Most important of all – follow the instructions and complete all the tasks you are given to do.

in the in-tray of the specified role level in terms of variety, complexity and volume of detail. These can include organisational charts, diary entries, emails, letters, invoices, statistics, product information, staff issues, meetings and complaint letters.

These exercises are not as straightforward as they look and it is important that you identify the possible linkages across items and make decisions where necessary. If asked to instruct or delegate to others, you need to make your recommendations and actions clear and succinct.

In-tray exercises are predominantly completed in paper-based format although there are some available that are computer-based and involve dealing with a range of emails and electronic information. In some circumstances you are also required to highlight if you think items are low, medium or high priority. Make sure you do this as they are assessing your skills in prioritisation.

In-tray exercises can range from 45 minutes to two hours.

Case study

Some organisations use a case study approach that forms the core of the assessment centre where all of the exercises relate to a specific business scenario. For the purposes of the exercises you are often asked to assume a specific role within the organisation.

You are likely to be given a document at the beginning of the assessment day that will contain a range of background information that you will need to refer to during completion of all the exercises. You will have an allotted amount of time to read the documents and make any notes, while retaining this document and your notes for use and reference purposes throughout the assessment centre.

This is a challenging situation and don't underestimate the pressure you will be under. Some assessment centres don't necessarily give you specific time slots to complete some of the exercises, particularly written or analysis exercises, and leave you to find the time throughout the day. Consider the following:

● Keep your background briefing document with you at all times.
● Make sure you are familiar with your timetable for the day to give yourself as much time as you can.
● Don't be lulled into spending lots of time talking with other candidates.
● Keep focused on what you have to do.
● Be yourself – although you are being asked to take the role of someone in the business scenario you are not being asked to act.

Fact-find exercises

A fact-find exercise is completed individually, but you need to interact with an assessor/actor to gain the relevant information. For this part of an assessment you are likely to be allocated a period of planning time where you are given an overview of the immediate circumstances around an incident. This could be anything from 5 to 15 minutes.

Following this planning time you will then have access to a 'resource person' who will have information related to your brief. During this time you will be required to ask a range of questions to elicit key pieces of information and make a decision or recommendation based on this information. You will then be required to present your decision or recommendations to the resource person. During this time, he or she may challenge your views and ask questions about your rationale. This discussion with the resource person will generally take around 30 minutes.

TOP TIPS

● Use your preparation time to the best effect; for example, highlight all the relevant and key pieces of information.
● Make a clear list of the questions you want to ask and the information you need to obtain.
● Use open questions – how, what, why, when and where.
● Avoid using closed questions as you may then only get one-word answers or a simple 'yes' or 'no', which may be no use to you at all.
● Make a clear decision and give a depth of rationale.
● Avoid sitting on the fence. If you do, make sure you have good reasons to back this up.
● Don't forget to build a rapport with the resource person – they may well be assessing your interpersonal skills so avoid making them feel as though they are being interrogated.

In addition to the discussion you could be asked to present a written summary of your decision, giving details of your rationale.

This exercise is designed to assess your ability to deal with stressful situations and your skills in judgement, planning and organising, problem analysis, decisiveness and oral communication.

Presentation

Presentation topics vary widely and will obviously be dependent upon the job you are applying for. Some will ask you to talk about a project or a piece of work you have completed, how you did this, what you did, how you contributed and how successful this was. Others may ask to you talk about how you plan to approach your first three months in the new role. There are generally two forms of presentation.

Pre-prepared

This is where you are given the presentation topic prior to attending the assessment centre. Clear instructions will be given, with a title, length of presentation time and what resources will be available on the day, for instance, flipchart or PowerPoint/projector. In some situations there may be no resources available; if this is the case, make sure you take handouts.

REMEMBER!

If you fail to plan your presentation properly, you are planning to fail.

Prepared on the day

You will be given a presentation topic, allocated preparation time and resources in order to plan and prepare a presentation. You will then be asked to present this to an audience at an allotted time during the day.

TOP TIPS
- Check beforehand how many people you will be presenting to.
- Check the length of time that your presentation should be and stick to it.
- Ensure your presentation has a beginning, middle and end.
- Consider the audience you are presenting to and what they will be interested in.
- Ensure your slides or handouts are clear and concise. If there is too much information in them, your audience may struggle to follow you and you will lose their attention.
- Take at least three copies of your presentation to hand out to your audience.
- Introduce yourself at the beginning and ensure you summarise at the end.
- Grab the attention of the audience at the beginning if you feel comfortable doing so.
- Thank the audience at the end and ask if there are any questions.
- Practise, practise and practise! Say the presentation out loud when you practise.

Role play/interactive or simulation exercises

This type of exercise usually simulates a situation that you are likely to have to deal with in the role you are applying for. Despite the fact that candidates sometimes feel it is 'play acting', role-play exercises are a very good indicator of how you would normally react and deal with such situations.

Role plays, interactive or simulation exercises cover a variety of situations, from dealing with issues relating to staff, such as performance reviews, counselling, disciplinary or grievance, to more externally related situations, such as difficult customers, negotiating contracts, selling a product or service, and building relationships. There are also situations where you may have to meet with more than one person; for instance, conduct a team briefing or meeting with your new team.

These types of exercises are becoming increasingly popular within recruitment situations and are often used as an additional exercise to run alongside an interview as well as part of a full assessment at an assessment centre.

It is likely that you will be given a full brief of instructions surrounding the situation and the individual(s) you are going to be meeting. You will be given a chance to read these and familiarise yourself with them within the preparation time,

REMEMBER!

The role players will react to how you deal with them. If someone is being unhelpful, this is on purpose to try to get you to talk more and ask further questions. You may need to open up the conversation further.

which could be anything from 10 to 30 minutes. Role-play meetings will then generally last around 20–45 minutes, dependent upon the nature of the situation.

You may find that you will be role playing with an actor or an experienced Human Resources person. There is likely to also be an additional person in the room who will be assessing your performance.

TOP TIPS

- Read through the brief carefully and highlight the key facts.
- Make notes of how you want to approach the meeting.
- Take your notes into the meeting – you may not remember everything in the heat of the moment.
- Make notes during the meeting of what is agreed – but don't become too preoccupied with this.
- Take ownership of setting up the room for how you would like it. For example, move chairs if this is needed.
- Avoid positioning yourself so a table is between you and the role player. Instead, sit across the corner of a desk to create a more open environment for the meeting.
- Ensure you make good eye contact with the role player.
- Be aware of your body language. For example, sit upright, face the person, don't fold your arms, don't slouch, use nodding and smiling to encourage communication (see page 14).

Scheduling exercises

These exercises are designed to assess your ability to deal with the scheduling of activities or resources. You will be given a range of information to analyse and asked to prepare a plan indicating how resources should be allocated to meet a set deadline or specific objective.

These exercises range in level of difficulty dependent upon the position you are applying for. You will be asked to take into account priority of actions, tasks that can run in parallel, timescales, diary availability and contingencies.

Scenarios could range from scheduling production of goods to arranging a sales conference. You will be given a specific timescale to complete the exercise, which could range from 30 minutes to one-and-a-half hours, dependent upon the complexity of the situation.

Generally these exercises will assess areas such as attention to detail, planning and organising, prioritisation and problem analysis together with decision making.

TOP TIPS

- Read through the information carefully first, before you put pen to paper.
- Identify and remove any irrelevant information.
- Identify the links between items; they will be there.
- Draw out a plan on rough paper first.
- Use all of the resources available to you.

Interview

See pages 10–16 for preparation advice and all related previous chapters for addressing questions and how to answer these.

Psychometric tests

The name 'psychometric tests' covers a variety of tests that include:

- Ability tests: to assess your ability in specific areas.
- Aptitude tests: to assess your skill level in job-specific areas, such as negotiation or management.
- Personality questionnaires: to show how you work and your personality.
- Motivational questionnaires: to assess what drives you in your work.

When these tests are first encountered, some candidates find the thought of completing them daunting, but it is all a matter of knowing what to expect and how to prepare for them. Psychometric testing will help you to:

- Demonstrate your strengths.
- Be assessed fairly on job-relevant criteria.
- Find out more about your strengths and development needs.
- Make future career decisions based on your abilities.

Psychometric testing will help employers to:

- Select people best suited to the demands of the job.
- Identify areas where individuals might benefit from further development.
- Obtain objective information about people's abilities and preferences.

Ability and aptitude tests

Employers often use aptitude assessments as part of their assessment procedures for the selection and development of staff. Research has shown that they are powerful predictors of performance at work and hence are becoming increasingly popular. They are not linked to general knowledge and focus on assessing your ability to reason with information and make logical decisions. Some of the more common tests are:

- Verbal reasoning/analysis/comprehension
- Numerical reasoning/analysis /comprehension
- Spatial awareness
- Diagrammatical analysis
- Clerical checking
- Mechanical reasoning
- Critical thinking.

Some companies use these tests as a screening process. They have a minimum score as a pass mark and if you reach this, then your application is likely to proceed further. If not, it is likely that your application will stop there.

Some of these tests are completed online, so you may be asked to complete these prior to attending an interview or assessment centre. You will be emailed a web link and password and asked to complete the test before a certain cut-off date. Full instructions are provided. It is important that when you complete this test, that you do it and not someone else. You may well be re-tested at interview and you could fall flat on your face if your friend the maths genius completed your numerical test for you. Also, organisations that provide these tests have mechanisms that make it difficult for you to cheat.

Preparing for aptitude tests

You should be told prior to attending that you are being asked to complete some tests. It is best practice for organisations to send you a practice leaflet prior to attending or give you the web link of the organisation who is supplying the tests. It is advisable to do the practice questions as these can give you a really good insight into what you will be asked to do.

Do:

● Undertake the practice tests in advance, either online or using the practice leaflet sent to you.
● Ask for a practice leaflet if you haven't been sent one.
● Ask what specific tests you will be completing and how; for example, will it be paper based, computer based or online?
● Ask how the test results will be used.
● Remember your glasses if you need them.
● Make the assessment centre aware in advance if you have a condition that may inhibit your ability to do the test, such as any sight conditions, dyslexia or inability to use a keyboard.
● Ask when and how you can get some feedback on your results.

Taking the test

Most ability tests are taken under exam conditions, so don't be surprised if you walk into a room that has been laid out in this way. Timings for tests can range from five minutes to one hour. You will be given all of the resources that you need, such as pen, pencil, rough paper and calculator.

TOP TIPS

● Make sure you can see a clock and note the start and finish time.
● Don't spend too long over any one question.
● If you can't work an answer out, move on to the next question, there may be time to go back at the end and think about it further.

Assessment centres

Sample aptitude tests

Here are examples of verbal and numerical aptitude tests. To answer each question, simply tick against the option you have chosen. The answers for each test are given upside down at the foot of the pages.

Verbal analysis

Choose the best answer to each question from the options given, based only on the information in the following passage.

Consumer trends

Sticking to traditional eating times and formal eating habits is no longer the norm for most people. The value and number of on-the-run eating occasions, both snacks and meals, is increasing significantly. The three meals a day maxim no longer holds true because more consumers are eating outside of the home and at times to suit their lifestyles. Breakfast, in particular, is now more commonly skipped and those who do eat breakfast are taking less time to prepare it. Consumers are developing more complex and paradoxical eating patterns and demanding more convenience products, but ones that are healthier, i.e. guilt free indulgence.

1 **Eating on-the-run is increasing.**

A   True on the basis of the passage

B   False on the basis of the passage

C   Not possible to say if the statement is true or false on the basis of the passage

2 **Which one of the following would meet the emerging consumer demands described in the passage?**

A   Breakfast clubs

B   Cooking lessons

C   Healthy snacks

D   Nutritional advice

3 **Which one of the following provides the best summary of the main point of the passage?**

A   Eating habits have changed

B   Manufacturers need to produce healthier food

C   Meals and snacks need to be quick to prepare

D   People want to be able to eat quickly

4 **Which one of the following would best replace 'maxim' while maintaining the meaning of the passage?**

A   schedule

B   pattern

C   limit

D   principle

Numerical comprehension

Choose the best answer to each question relating to the table below.

Interview schedule

Session	Interview time slot (60 minutes per interview)	Number of candidates
Monday	09:30–10:30	3
	10:30–11:30	4
	11:30–12:30	2
Tuesday	09:30–10:30	5
	10:30–11:30	4
	11:30–12:30	2

1 More candidates are interviewed on Monday than on Tuesday

A True

B False

C Not possible to say

2 If two interviewers per candidate are required to carry out an interview, what is the maximum number of interviewers needed at any time?

A 8

B 10

C 12

D 14

E 16

3 If five of the applicants were hired, what would be the ratio of successful candidates to candidates interviewed?

A 1:5

B 1:4

C 1:2

D 4:1

E 5:1

4 A successful candidate is more likely to have been interviewed on Tuesday than on Monday.

A True

B False

C Not possible to say

Answers: 1B 2B 3B 4C

Personality questionnaires

Personality questionnaires assess personal behavioural preferences – how you like to work. They do not assess your abilities but are concerned with how you see yourself in the way you relate to others, approach solving problems and manage your emotions.

In this type of test there are no right or wrong answers – the employer is using the questionnaire to find out more about you as a person, understand what makes you tick, assess your suitability for the role and maybe explore any areas of concern further at the interview.

What to expect

Many personality questionnaires can be completed online so you may be asked to complete it prior to attending an interview or assessment centre. You will be emailed a web link and password and asked to complete the questionnaire before a certain cut-off date. Full instructions are provided. It is important that when you complete this test, that you do it and not someone else. They want to find out about you.

Alternatively, you will be asked to complete a paper-based questionnaire on the day – there is usually no time limit for completion, but it will probably be done in exam conditions in a room with other candidates. You should be told prior to attending that you are being asked to complete a personality questionnaire.

There are essentially two formats to personality questionnaires. In the first format, you are asked to rate yourself on a series of statements and state whether you agree or disagree with the statement about you. In the second format, you are asked to choose between different statements indicating which description is least or most like you. All the statements look at different aspects of personality.

TOP TIPS

- Complete the questionnaire without pondering at any great length over the answers – the answer that first comes to mind when you read the question is probably the one that is most accurate about you before you have had time to rationalise this choice or decide whether or not it is a quality you like about yourself.
- Don't try to double guess what aspect of personality the questionnaire is exploring with a particular question – the chances are you will be wrong.
- Don't try to manipulate the result to appear the kind of person you think the employer would like to see – there are double checks in these questionnaires to identify such practice.
- Ensure you complete all the questions.
- Try to avoid 'unsure' as a rating unless absolutely unavoidable.
- Don't go back over your answers at the end – you may be tempted to change some of them.

Sample personality questionnaire

The questionnaire is presented in blocks of six statements, which you are asked to rate on a nine-point scale, ranging from 'Very strongly disagree' to 'Very strongly agree'. Please mark your responses against the appropriate rating scale for each statement.

	Very strongly disagree	Strongly disagree	Disagree	Slightly disagree	Unsure	Slightly agree	Agree	Strongly agree	Very strongly agree
It is **important** to me to know how well I have done									✓
I **am** an optimist									✓
I am **good** at generating ideas			✓						
Using technology is one of my **strong** points					✓				
I am **good at** understanding how others feel								✓	
I am someone who **is** confident when meeting new people								✓	

In the example, the respondent has indicated that they:
- **very strongly agree** that it is *important* to know how well they have done
- **very strongly agree** that they *are* an optimist
- **disagree** that they are *good at* generating ideas
- are **unsure** whether or not technology is one of their strong points
- **strongly agree** that they are *good at* understanding how others feel
- **strongly agree** that they are someone who is confident when meeting new people

Other than familiarising yourself with a few online samples of personality questionnaires there is really no preparation that you need to do prior to completing a personality questionnaire – it is not a test, just a way for the employer to find out more about you. It can be helpful to ask the employer the following questions:

- How will they use the output from the questionnaire?
- Can you have feedback from the questionnaire results?

Motivational questionnaires

These are a type of personality questionnaire and are constructed and administered in exactly the same way. Instead of looking at the full range of personality traits they focus upon understanding the situations that increase or decrease an individual's motivation at work. As with a personality questionnaire there are no right or wrong answers.

Employers use these questionnaires in selection situations to identify whether the type of work and culture of the organisation appear to be suitable for you. As with a personality questionnaire, the results should always be explored further at the interview rather than just taken at face value.

Whether completed online or in a paper-based format, you will be asked to rate a series of statements of how conditions or situations in the workplace could affect your motivation in a positive or negative manner.

There is really no preparation you can do for these tests – just be yourself and answer the questions as honestly as possible.

Belbin team roles

These may well help you in describing the role you take within a team and how you contribute to the team. A team role is a tendency to behave, contribute and interrelate with others in a particular way. Very few people display characteristics of just one team role; in fact, most people have three or four preferred roles, which can be adopted as the situation requires.

Team role	Contribution
Plant	<ul><li>Take a creative and imaginative approach to tasks</li><li>May be fairly unorthodox</li><li>Like to solve problems – see the links</li></ul>
Resource investigator	<ul><li>Fairly extroverted in your style</li><li>Enthusiastic and enjoy communicating with people</li><li>Like to explore different opportunities and develop contacts outside of the team</li></ul>
Co-ordinator	<ul><li>Likely to be fairly mature, confident and a good leader or chair</li><li>Likely to clarify goals, promote decision making and delegate to others in order to achieve the task</li></ul>
Shaper	<ul><li>Likely be challenging of others</li><li>Dynamic in your style</li><li>Thrive on the pressure</li><li>Have the drive and courage to overcome obstacles</li></ul>
Monitor evaluator	<ul><li>Fairly sober in your style</li><li>Prefer to take a more strategic perspective – be discerning</li><li>Likely to see all of the options available</li><li>Have good judgement</li></ul>
Team worker	<ul><li>Likely to be co-operative when working with others</li><li>Have a mild and perceptive approach – diplomatic</li><li>Listen to the ideas of others</li><li>Build relationships and avert friction within the team</li></ul>
Implementer	<ul><li>Take a disciplined approach</li><li>Reliable, conservative in your approach and efficient</li><li>Turn ideas into practical actions</li></ul>
Completer finisher	<ul><li>Likely to be painstaking, conscientious and see the task through</li><li>Look for errors and omissions</li><li>Deliver work within timescales</li></ul>
Specialist	<ul><li>Take a single-minded approach</li><li>Self-starting and dedicated</li><li>Likely to provide technical knowledge and skills</li></ul>

Key words: attributes and qualities

Here is a list of key skills, attributes and qualities that may help you in preparing answers to questions that focus on 'What skills have you learnt or developed?' or 'What can you bring to this role?'

Articulate	Motivated
Change orientated	Negotiator
Communicator	Organiser
Confident	Passionate
Confidential	Persuasive
Customer focused	Planner
Deadline focused	Practical
Decision maker	Prioritisation
Diplomatic	Proactive
Encouraging	Problem solver
Energetic	Reactive
Enthusiastic	Responsible
Forward thinking	Self-motivated
Influential	Supportive
Initiative	Team worker
Innovative	Theoretical
Leader	

Useful addresses

Careers Northern Ireland
Tel: 028 9044 1781
www.careersserviceni.com

Careers Scotland
Tel: 0845 850 2502
www.careers-scotland.org.uk

Careers Wales
Tel: 0800 100 900
www.careerswales.com
or www.gyrfacymru.com

Chartered Institute of Personnel and Developments
151 The Broadway
London SW19 1JQ
Tel: 020 8612 6200
www.cipd.co.uk

Childcare Link
Tel: 08000 96 02 96
www.childcarelink.gov.uk
(Government-funded strategy to help people back into the workplace by removing the childcare barrier)

Citizens Advice Bureau (CAB)
Check telephone directory for local office
www.adviceguide.org.uk

Companies House
Crown Way
Maindy
Cardiff CF14 3UZ
Tel: 0870 33 33 636
www.companieshouse.gov.uk

Connexions Direct
Tel: 080 800 13219
www.connexions-direct.com
(Careers advice)

Employment Opportunities for People With Disabilities
53 New Broad Street
London EC2M 1SL
Tel: 020 7448 5420
www.opportunities.org.uk

Jobcentre Plus
Tel: 0845 606 0234
Textphone: 0800 023 4888
www.jobcentreplus.gov.uk

Jobseeker Direct
Tel: 0845 6060 234
Textphone: 0845 6055 255

Recruitment and Employment Confederation
36–38 Mortimer Street
London W1W 7RG
Tel: 020 7462 3260
www.rec.uk.com

Surestart
Sure Start Unit
Department for Education and Skills and Department for Work and Pensions
Level 2, Caxton House
Tothill Street
London SW1H 9NA
Tel: 0870 000 2288
www.surestart.gov.uk

Index

Index

Index

which?

Which? magazine

Which? magazine has a simple goal in life – to offer truly independent advice to consumers that they can genuinely trust – from which credit card to use through to which washing machine to buy. Every month the magazine is packed with 84 advertisement-free pages of expert advice on the latest products. It takes on the biggest of businesses on behalf of all consumers and is not afraid to tell consumers to avoid their products. Truly the consumer champion. To subscribe, go to www.which.co.uk.

Which? Online

www.which.co.uk gives you access to all Which? content online and much, much more. It's updated regularly, so you can read hundreds of product reports and Best Buy recommendations, keep up to date with Which? campaigns, compare products, use our financial planning tools and search for the best cars on the market. You can also access reviews from *The Good Food Guide*, register for email updates and browse our online shop – so what are you waiting for? To subscribe, go to www.which.co.uk.

Which? Legal Service

Which? Legal Service offers immediate access to first-class legal advice at unrivalled value. One low-cost annual subscription allows members to enjoy unlimited legal advice by telephone on a wide variety of legal topics, including consumer law – problems with goods and services, employment law, holiday problems, neighbour disputes, parking tickets, clamping fines and tenancy advice for private residential tenants in England and Wales. To subscribe, call 01992 822 828 or go to www.whichlegalservice.co.uk.

which?

CV and Interview Handbook
Sue Tumelty
ISBN: 978 1 84490 047 3
Price: £10.99

Changing jobs or embarking on a new career can be one of life's stressful events. This guide looks at the all-important CV, how to interpret job adverts, what you should and shouldn't say in a job interview and much more. *CV and Interview Handbook* takes you through the job-hunting process from application to assessment centres and your first week at work.

Tax Handbook 2009/10
Tony Levene
ISBN: 978 1 84490 060 2
Price: £10.99

Make sense of the complicated rules, legislation and red tape with *Tax Handbook 2009/10*. Written by personal finance journalist and award-winning consumer champion Tony Levene, this guide gives expert advice on all aspects of the UK tax system and does the legwork for you. It includes information on finding the right accountant and how to get the best from them, NI contributions, VAT and tax credits for families. This new edition also contains updates from the 2009 Budget, disability credits, tax advice on cars, the latest news on the Taxpayers' Charter and step-by-step advice on completing the self-assessment form.

Pension Handbook
Jonquil Lowe
ISBN: 978 1 84490 025 1
Price: £9.99

A definitive guide to sorting out your pension, whether you are deliberating over SERPs/S2Ps, organising a personal pension or moving schemes. Cutting through confusion and dispelling apathy, Jonquil Lowe provides up-to-date advice on how to maximise your savings and provide for the future.

Which? Books

Which? Books get to the heart of subjects that really matter. We offer impartial, expert advice on savings and investments, pensions and retirement, property, making the most of your money and major life events. As the job market stumbles, we have advice on CVs and interviews and how to turn your idea into a thriving business.

For some light relief and recreation, we also publish the country's most trusted restaurant guide, *The Good Food Guide*. Every year we bring you the latest reviews, foodie features and top tips for budget eats. To find out more about Which? Books, visit www.which.co.uk or call 01903 828557.

"Which? tackles the issues that really matter to consumers and gives you the right advice and active support you need to buy the right products."